Writing Books
for
Young People

Books for Young People

BY JAMES CROSS GIBLIN

Writing Books
for
Young People

Revised and Expanded Edition

by James Cross Giblin

Publishers   THE WRITER, INC.   *Boston*

Brief excerpts from the following books are reprinted by permission of Clarion Books, a Houghton Mifflin Company Imprint.

Daphne's Book by Mary Downing Hahn. Copyright © 1983 by Mary Downing Hahn; *Scary, Scary Halloween* by Eve Bunting and Jan Brett. Text copyright © 1986 by Eve Bunting; *So Many Cats!* by Beatrice Schenk de Regniers and Ellen Weiss. Text copyright © 1985 by Beatrice Schenk de Regniers; *The Half-Birthday Party* by Charlotte Pomerantz and DyAnne DiSalvo-Ryan. Text copyright © 1984 by Charlotte Pomerantz; and *Dark and Full of Secrets* by Carol Carrick and Donald Carrick. Text copyright © 1984 by Carol Carrick.

Portions of this book appeared previously in *The Writer, Horn Book, The Basics of Writing for Children,* and *Children's Writer.*

Library of Congress Cataloging-in-Publication Data

Giblin, James.
    Writing books for young people / by James Cross Giblin.—Rev. and expanded ed.
      p. cm.
    ISBN 0-87116-175-3 :
    1. Children's literature—Authorship. I. Title.
PN147.5.G5 1995
808.06'8—dc20
                                    94-39243
                                        CIP

ACKNOWLEDGMENTS

Special thanks go to the authors and illustrators whose work I have edited, and from whom I have learned so much. Among them are: Carole S. Adler, Ursula Arndt, Edna Barth, Marion Dane Bauer, Jan Brett, Roy Brown, Eve Bunting, Carol and Donald Carrick, Arthur Catherall, Kay Chorao, Eileen Christelow, Dick Gackenbach, Paul Galdone, Mary Downing Hahn, Anna Grossnickle Hines, Mildred Lee, J. J. McCoy, Arnold Madison, Jim Murphy, Lila Perl, Stella Pevsner, Robert Quackenbush, Beatrice Schenk de Regniers, Ron Roy, Gloria Skurzynski, Carla Stevens, Jane Resh Thomas, Margot Tomes, Patricia Willis, Jane Yolen.

Thanks, too, to the editors I've had the privilege of working with: Patricia H. Allen, John Brady, Dorothy Briley, Deborah Brodie, William Brohaugh, Kent L. Brown, Jr., A. S. Burack, Sylvia K. Burack, Marianne Carus, Beatrice Creighton, Barbara Fenton, Lillian N. Gerhardt, Ethel L. Heins, Dianne Hess, Elizabeth Isele, Antonia Markiet, Sidney Phillips, Norma Jean Sawicki, Anita Silvey, Susan M. Tierney, Ann Troy.

Above all, I want to pay tribute to my late mother, Anna Cross Giblin, who was responsible for introducing me to children's books and reading.

For Sue Alexander

CONTENTS

Author's Note

To avoid awkwardness, I have used the word "he" rather than "he or she." I trust readers will understand that I intend this use of "he" to be taken in the generic sense.

—J. C. G.

Writing Books
for
Young People

1

Getting Ready to Write

YOU'VE DECIDED you want to write a book for children, but you don't know how to get started. Or perhaps you're an established writer who isn't sure just where the children's book field is headed. Whichever the case, you sign up for one of the hundreds of writers' conferences in children's literature that are held throughout the year in virtually every state in the union.

I've spoken as an editor and author at many such conferences, from Los Angeles, California, and Portland, Oregon, to Northampton, Massachusetts, and Sarasota, Florida, but no matter the location, the questions the conferees ask are always the same:

- What are the latest trends in juvenile fiction?

- How can I tell if a nonfiction topic is worth writing about?

- Should I get an illustrator for my picture book story before I submit the manuscript?

- Do I need an agent?

This book was written to answer these and many similar questions. It explores the three major types of writing for children—fiction, nonfiction, and picture books—lists the requirements of each field, and describes some of the pitfalls to avoid in your writing. It discusses the basic problems that all writers must solve for themselves: How do you get an idea? Once you have one, how do you develop it into a satisfying manuscript? And then, how do you market the manuscript successfully?

Before getting into that, however, it helps to have a bit of background on the size and scope of the market. Children's book publishing in America is a big business that nets annually over $1 billion in hardcover sales and $500 million in paperback sales. The majority of hardcover sales—perhaps as much as 75%—are made to public and school libraries, but there's a growing market for juvenile hardcovers as well as paperbacks in bookstore chains and in specialized children's bookstores. Books of all types and for all age groups are in demand, ranging from board books about colors and shapes for one-year-olds to probing novels for teenagers.

To meet this demand, over five thousand new juvenile titles are published each year. While the bulk of these are written by established authors, there's room on every children's book publisher's list for newcomers with a fresh and original approach, writers who show promise of developing into the established authors of tomorrow. Perhaps one of these new authors will be you. But first you'll need to decide what you want to say, and to which youthful audience, and then you'll have to learn how to say it in the most effective way possible.

"There's so much I want to write about, but I just can't seem to find the time," is an excuse I often hear from would-be writers. I'm afraid I don't have much patience with it—or them. "You'll never *find* the time to write," I reply. "You'll have to *make* the time, and on a regular basis." No matter how busy you are, there must be a few hours a week that you can devote to your writing.

Those hours will probably involve sacrifices of one kind or another. You may have to decline an appealing invitation to a Sunday brunch with old friends if it cuts into your writing time. Or you may have to miss that fascinating late-night talk show interview if you're going to hold to your self-imposed schedule and get up at five in the morning to work on your children's book.

While it's a good idea to set aside some time to write each day, it often isn't possible, and isn't absolutely necessary. What's more important is to look hard at your weekly schedule and decide on a certain number of hours when—barring vacations or sudden emergencies—you're pretty sure you'll be able to sit at your writing desk. They may add up to two hours on Tuesday, a half hour on Thursday, a full hour on Friday, and another hour on Sunday. It really doesn't matter as long as the schedule is realistic and you hold to it rigorously. Even if you have only three or four hours a week for writing at first, you'll be surprised at how much you can accomplish if you work at it steadily.

Besides time to write, every author also needs a place where he can be alone to concentrate and give free rein to his ideas. It doesn't have to be a separate room just for that purpose, and usually isn't. Over the years I've heard of one author who moved her desk to the laundry room, next to the washing machine, and another who put his in the tool shed alongside the garage. The essential thing is that it be a place where you can be by yourself. And don't be afraid to hang a "Don't Disturb" sign on the door. If you don't take your writing time seriously, no one else in your life will.

After you've settled on a place to write and established a definite writing schedule, how can you best get started? Every author has his own favorite recipe for warming up. Some simply switch on their word processor or put a sheet of paper in the typewriter and plunge into notes, an outline, or even Chapter One. Others straighten their desks and sharpen pencils to get into the mood. Still others draw floor plans of the rooms they'll be describing in their novel or sketch the faces and clothes of the main characters.

Whatever works best for you as a trigger, I strongly recommend that you keep a writing notebook and/or a journal. Before I began to write articles for publication, and later juvenile nonfiction books, I used my journal to sharpen my writing skills. I might not pick up the journal for weeks or even months, but when I did I recorded in it the main events in my life, what was delighting me and what was troubling me. Although I didn't intend for anyone else to read the journal, I tried to organize each entry in the clearest and most effective way, and polished every sentence until its rhythm satisfied me. Keeping such a journal would probably be useful for you, too, if you're not sure how to get started with your writing or are between book projects.

After I began writing books steadily, I maintained my personal journal but also started a series of writing notebooks. Since then they've become a sort of continuing logbook of my writing career. In them I outline books, articles, and lectures, draft complicated letters before typing them, and make lists of my various free-lance commitments and when I plan to get to them. You might use a similar workbook to jot down ideas for new novels or picture books as they occur to you, or to write brief character sketches of two teenage girls you over-hear on a bus or a little boy you see walking a big dog. You never know when you may be able to weave such an incident into a story.

Another good use for a notebook, especially for begin-ning authors, is for writing brief critiques of children's books you read. I'm always surprised, when I go through a pile of unsolicited submissions in my office or evaluate manuscripts at a writers' conference, by the fact that so many new authors seem almost completely unaware of what's being published in the children's book field today. They may remember a few books they them-selves read and loved as children, and some others that they read aloud to their own children twenty years ago. But they obviously haven't taken the trouble to read any *current* children's books before they sat down at their word processors. As a consequence, most of their manu-scripts are unsuited to today's audience.

Would a doctor perform an operation before learning the basic techniques of surgery or a tailor cut out the cloth for a garment without first making a pattern? Obvi-ously, a children's book writer can't expect to be able to dash off a successful story without reading any contem-porary children's books. If you'd like expert guidance on what to read, ask your local children's librarian for a list of recommended titles. Or you can go to one of the children's bookstores that have sprung up all over the country in the last decade or so. The buyer can tell you which books children especially like, from board books for tots to young adult novels in paperback.

After you've read and thought about a book, you may want to write a brief description of it in your notebook, and analyze where you feel the author succeeded with his plotting and characterization, and where he failed. By doing so, you'll hone your critical skills. You'll also gain some valuable insights into the craft of writing that particular kind of book.

As you delve into the wide range of contemporary children's literature, from picture books for preschoolers to biographies for middle-grade readers to novels for young teens, begin thinking of where you might fit into the picture as an author. What age group would you feel most comfortable writing for? A juvenile editor I know believes that all children's book authors are cases of arrested development. He's joking, of course, but there may be more than a little truth in his statement. Picture book authors like Charlotte Zolotow, James Stevenson, and Beatrice Schenk de Regniers clearly have a direct link to their memories of what it was like to be five years old, while to such popular young adult novelists as Judy Blume, Robert Cormier, and Paula Danziger, the agonies of adolescence are as vivid as if they'd happened yesterday.

Close identification with a particular age group isn't limited to writers of fiction. For example, as an author of nonfiction I almost always write for the eight-to-twelve-year-old audience, the "middle-aged" group, as it's called. I'm convinced that's because those were my happiest years as a child, a time when the world and its history opened up for me and I felt as if I were making an exciting new discovery each day. Now I'm writing out of my memories of that boy and for the thousands of children who, I hope, share his interests and enthusiasms.

In determining which age group is right for you, you might ask yourself some of the following questions: (1) What would I most like to write? A fantasy about a talking pig? An account of the extinction of the dinosaurs? A novel about a girl with a weight problem who's afraid no one will ask her to the prom? (2) Why do I want to work with this material? Does it spring from some of my own experiences, pleasures, fears, or fascinations as a child or adolescent? and (3) What age group do I think would be most interested in my book?

Be honest in your answers. Especially with a first book, don't pretend to be interested in something you're not just because you think it has a better chance of selling. Maybe your friends advised you to write a romance because all the teenage girls they know are reading novels about young love, but if you really want to explore the feelings of a lonely little boy in first grade, trust your instincts. A more moving, and salable, manuscript will probably be the result.

In the course of getting ready to write, many authors wonder what sort of equipment to buy. Should they use a trusty old portable typewriter or purchase a sleek new electronic model? Or should they make the big leap and invest in an expensive computer and top-quality printer? As with deciding which age group to write for, my advice is to get the equipment you feel most comfortable with. If you like to compose directly on the typewriter, but hate the drudgery of retyping page after page of revisions, then a computer would probably be a time-saver for you. But if, like me, you prefer to write in longhand and type the manuscript only as the final step, then a computer might not be necessary.

When making your final choice of equipment, just remember one thing: *No pen or typewriter or word processor was ever responsible for the success or failure of a manuscript.* That depends entirely on the writer who uses it, and the ideas in his or her head.

All right. Let's turn now from general advice to a specific writing situation. Imagine that you're a young man or woman who wants to write for children. It's Tuesday morning at 5:30, and the rest of the family is still asleep. You have an hour-and-a-half before you have to leave for your job in the city or get the children off to school. So you go quietly to the table in the sunroom that you've made into a desk and take out your writing notebook.

In the last few months, you've been reading one children's book after another. After studying them carefully and pondering your own talents and interests, you've decided you'd like to write nonfiction for the upper elementary age group. Now the moment of truth has arrived: You have to settle on an idea to explore. What will it be? As if looking to nature for inspiration, you gaze out the window at the azalea bushes which are about to burst into bloom. Maybe children would be interested in an up-to-date book on gardening. . . .

Where *do* good nonfiction ideas come from, and how can they be shaped into exciting and marketable books? Those are the questions we'll take up and try to answer in the next three chapters.

2

Finding Good Ideas for Juvenile Nonfiction Books

NONFICTION HAS ALWAYS been a staple of children's book publishing, since youngsters in each new generation have wanted to find out the facts about everything for school assignments, or just to satisfy their curiosity. And it's interesting to note that the first John Newbery Medal (which recognizes excellence in children's literature) was awarded in 1922 to a work of nonfiction, Hendrik Willem Van Loon's *The Story of Mankind*.

For many years after that, however, nonfiction books tended to be Cinderellas on many publishers' lists. There the books were, sitting quietly in the background with titles like *The Wonders of Light* and *Clara Barton: Civil War Nurse*, while the bulk of the publishers' editorial, design, and promotion efforts were lavished on their fiction and picture book offerings. Juvenile nonfiction also suffered a heavy blow in the 1970s when federal funds for school libraries, probably the largest purchasers of nonfiction books, were sharply reduced. As a consequence, many publishers cut back on the number of new nonfiction titles they issued, and hundreds of solid backlist titles went out of print as sales declined.

This situation reversed itself in the 1980s when Cinderella suddenly found herself invited to a spectacular new nonfiction ball. Schoolchildren still needed information books, and there were fresh library funds to purchase them in many localities. Specialized children's bookstores provided a new market for juvenile nonfiction, especially for books aimed at preschoolers and early elementary age children.

Perhaps most important, reviewers and librarians began to treat juvenile nonfiction more seriously. *The Boston Globe-Horn Book* children's book awards set up a separate category to recognize the best nonfiction books. The Society of Children's Book Writers and Illustrators initiated a Golden Kite Award for nonfiction. The American Library Association, in successive years, named Rhoda Blumberg's *Commodore Perry in the Land of the Shogun* and Patricia Lauber's *Volcano: The Eruption and Healing of Mount St. Helens* as Newbery Honor Books, and then, in 1988, the A.L.A. awarded the Newbery Medal to Russell Freedman's *Lincoln: A Photobiography*—the first time a nonfiction book had received the coveted Newbery since 1956.

Today, and in the years ahead, all signs point to a wider range of juvenile nonfiction titles being made available to young readers. Many will appear in series like those published by Franklin Watts and Children's

Press. These series deal with all sorts of subjects, from the history and geography of each state, to discussions of contemporary social issues such as drugs, to how-to books on various sports, both established and new. If you're interested in doing a book for a series, you should study the publishers' catalogues and publications and then write the editors for information on their plans so that you can see where your idea might fit in.

Besides such series, most children's book publishers are offering an equally wide range of individual nonfiction titles for all age groups. There are colorful nonfiction picture books for preschoolers on everything from ants to icebergs; pure science, natural history, holiday, and social history titles for the middle grades; self-help and how-to books for older children and teenagers; and biographies for all age groups.

Whether a nonfiction book is part of a series or an individual title, chances are that it will be conceived and written in a way very different from the one that prevailed even a short while ago. Take, for instance, a book that I edited in the 1970s, *Juvenile Justice* by Willard A. Heaps. This book was typical of many nonfiction titles of its time. Designed for readers of junior-high age and up, it presented a broad overview of the entire juvenile justice system from the time a young person commits a crime until his or her case is decided and punishment is determined. The book was 224 pages long; fourteen actual case histories were woven into the text, and it included a list of sources and readings and an index. But it had no illustrations.

Juvenile Justice received excellent reviews in the library media, went through four printings, and was counted a solid success. But it's unlikely that a publisher would produce the book in the same style and manner today.

Why not? Because times have changed, and with them the way in which authors and publishers approach juvenile nonfiction topics. If Willard Heaps were planning a similar book now, he'd probably team up with a photographer, and they might decide to focus on one day's activities in a typical juvenile court. Or they might follow a single juvenile offender through the whole process, from apprehension, to trial, to disposal of the case.

Whichever course they chose, the basic facts about the juvenile justice system would emerge at appropriate points in the text. But the new manuscript would be tight; instead of over two hundred pages, it would probably run to no more than fifty pages. There would be at least one photograph on every double-page spread, and sometimes two or three. And the finished book would be only sixty-four or ninety-six pages long.

These hypothetical concepts point up three features that seem to be characteristic of the new approach to juvenile nonfiction, and that authors should keep firmly in mind. They apply to books for all age groups, from preschool picture books to titles aimed at young adults. The three key features are: a close focus on one significant aspect of a topic that will also reveal other aspects; a concise, tightly written text that will catch and hold the interest of young readers; and a built-in emphasis on illustrations, whether they be photographs or drawings, or a combination of the two. The visual impact of nonfiction is especially important now, when books have to compete with so many other media for a young person's attention.

Getting the idea

Despite the new emphasis on the visual in all types of

juvenile nonfiction, the text—however brief—is still the key factor that determines the form of any book. And every good text begins with a good idea. Such ideas come from many different sources, depending on the author's personal background, interests, and areas of expertise.

For example, when Russell Freedman attended an exhibit of photographs of turn-of-the-century immigrant children at the New-York Historical Society, he was moved by their lively, animated expressions despite the harsh conditions in which many of them lived and worked. The pictures made him think of his grandparents and other relatives who had emigrated to the United States from Eastern Europe at about the same time. From this museum visit came the idea for Mr. Freedman's striking nonfiction book, *Immigrant Kids*.

Caroline Arnold got the idea for her book, *Pets Without Homes*, when she read an article in a Los Angeles newspaper about a young veterinarian who visited area schools, telling youngsters about her work in an animal shelter and bringing along some of the shelter's furry residents for the children to see and play with. Arnold, who had a science background and had written a number of books on scientific subjects, thought children would be interested in reading about what goes on in a typical animal shelter. She contacted the veterinarian and a new book was under way.

The author took the idea a step further, however, before she began the actual writing. Aware of the illustration possibilities in the material, she decided the book would make a good photo essay. The term photo essay came into use in the 1970s to describe a type of nonfiction book for middle-grade children and older readers in which the illustrations, usually photographs, play as important a role as the text, and must be of equally high quality. Once Arnold had settled on a photo-essay approach, she got in touch with Richard Hewett, the professional photographer she had worked with on other books, to see if he would be interested in collaborating with her on the project. He was enthusiastic about the idea, and together they developed *Pets Without Homes* from that point on.

Sometimes the idea for a nonfiction book comes along when an author least expects it. That's what happened to me in the case of my book, *Chimney Sweeps*. I was flying to Oklahoma City on business when the plane stopped in Chicago and a tall, rangy young man carrying what I thought was a musical instrument case took the seat next to me. We started to talk, and I discovered that the man—whose name was Christopher Curtis— was a chimney sweep, and his case contained samples of the special brushes for cleaning chimneys that he manufactured at his own small factory in Vermont. He was on his way to Oklahoma City to conduct a seminar for local sweeps on how to clean chimneys more efficiently.

Chris went on to tell me a little about the history of chimney sweeping and its revival as a profession in the last decade or so. In turn, I told him I was a writer of children's books, and that he'd fired my interest in chimney sweeps as a possible subject. We exchanged business cards, and a month or so later I wrote to tell him that I'd followed up on the idea and had started researching the book on chimney sweeps. I asked him if he'd be willing to read the manuscript for accuracy. He agreed to do so and volunteered to supply photographs of present-day sweeps that could be used (and were) as illustrations in the book.

According to an old English superstition, it's lucky to

meet a chimney sweep. Well, meeting Christopher Curtis was certainly lucky for me!

Is the idea worth pursuing?

After you have an idea for a book, the next thing to do is test it to see if it's worth pursuing. But first you should ask yourself a blunt question: Is this an idea to which I want to devote a year or more of my life? For it takes most authors at least six months to research a nonfiction book and another six months to write and rewrite it. That's a major commitment of time and energy, and not one to be made lightly.

If your answer is "yes," you should go on to examine the idea carefully and see if it has enough levels to make a good book. What do I mean by levels? Look at the idea for *Immigrant Kids*. Not only did it offer Russell Freedman the opportunity to explore the life of children in another time, but it also gave him a chance to investigate the dramatic story of American immigration, a subject every child studies in school at one time or another.

Or take *Chimney Sweeps*. When I got into preliminary research for that book, I discovered that besides the obvious human interest centering on the plight of child sweeps in 19th-century England, the subject touched on architectural and economic history, and it had played an important role in the passage of the first laws against child labor. Weaving these different levels together made *Chimney Sweeps* more interesting to write—and I believe it makes it more interesting for readers also.

Once your idea has passed the "levels" test, the next step is to check R. R. Bowker's annual *Subject Guide to Children's Books in Print*, available in the reference department of most libraries, to see what else is available on the subject. When I looked up chimney sweeps,

I was pleased to find that no other nonfiction treatments were in print. But when I looked up skyscrapers in preparation for *The Skyscraper Book* I was dismayed to see six other books listed. Upon examining the books, though, I realized that several of them were written for the picture book audience, whereas I intended mine for the 8–12 age group, and all of the books focused on *how* skyscrapers were constructed, while I planned to emphasize *why* and *by whom* they were built.

This brings up the importance of deciding on the right age group and slant for your nonfiction idea. Often a subject such as skyscrapers can be treated for either preschoolers or upper elementary and junior high readers; which you choose to write for may depend on what else is available, or your inclinations as a writer, or both.

By the same token, a subject like skyscrapers can be approached from many different angles. The trick is to find one compatible with your interests and skills that doesn't merely duplicate existing material. If you succeed in coming up with that combination, public and school librarians will probably find room in their budgets for your book, even if they already have several other books about skyscrapers or whatever.

In recent years, another factor has entered into librarians' decisions about what nonfiction books to buy. With the renewed emphasis on quality education, both school and public librarians are looking for new, well-written books to replace titles that are either out of date or no longer available. So if you want to write a book about beavers, say, but are discouraged when you find several old books about that animal on your library's shelves, don't abandon the idea immediately. First, check to see if those books are still in print. If they're not, libraries can't replace their existing copies, and there will probably be publishers interested in your book if you have the necessary background, skill, and imagination to write it. After weighing your idea carefully and examining the competition, the time will come when you'll have to decide whether or not to proceed with it. Try to be as honest as possible with yourself at this point; it'll save you a lot of trouble and disappointment later. If you feel the idea just isn't large enough for a book, don't despair. It may provide the basis for an excellent children's magazine article. If, on the other hand, you're more convinced than ever that it has the makings of a book, new questions arise. Should you research and write the entire manuscript before approaching a publisher, or should you query first to find out if an editor is interested in your idea?

If you're a beginner, a combination of the two would probably be the best course to take. You should do enough research to make sure there's sufficient material for a book. Then you'll need to write a full outline and draft one or two sample chapters to show how you intend to treat the subject. After that, you can send query letters to publishers and ask if they'd like to see your outline and chapters.

Writing a nonfiction query letter or proposal

Some query letters for nonfiction books strain for a dramatic beginning: "Can you imagine the devastation that would result if a major new earthquake struck southern California?" Others go on for four or five single-spaced typewritten pages in which every section of every chapter is described in minute detail.

As an editor, I tend to tune out on such letters, for I like a query letter to be factual, to the point, and no more than a page long. Teaser openings don't work with me; I prefer a straightforward approach like that in the following example:

Dear Mr. Giblin:

I have spent the last year researching the life of Mary Todd Lincoln and have just completed the outline and three sample chapters of a proposed biography of her for ages 10 to 14.

Much has been written for this age group about Abraham Lincoln, of course, including Russell Freedman's excellent biography. But after checking the latest edition of the *Subject Guide to Children's Books in Print*, and talking with our local school and public librarians, I could find only two other books about Mrs. Lincoln, and both came out quite some time ago.

In my sample chapters, I have tried to deal honestly with the complexities of Mary Lincoln's character, and have not concealed or whitewashed the neurotic side of her personality. However, in many other respects I consider her to be a heroine who played an important role during one of the most difficult periods in our history. Certainly she is a woman young readers should know about.

I have previously published biographical articles for children in *Cricket* and *Highlights*, but this is my first attempt at a book. Would you like to see my sample material? I enclose a stamped, self-addressed envelope for your convenience in replying.

That sort of query letter would get a favorable response from me—and I imagine from most editors—because the author obviously has a thoughtful, professional attitude. And, after reading his outline and sample chapters, we might feel confident enough about the project to offer him a contract. At that point, buoyed by our commitment, the author would be ready to proceed with in-depth research.

Once an author has become established as a nonfiction writer, the submission procedure is different. Then, instead of doing an outline and sample chapters and querying editors, the author writes a *proposal* for a book and sends it to an editor. What exactly is a proposal? Basically a two- or three-page description of the future book, indicating what the subject will be and how the author intends to treat it. Perhaps a sample of text, or a brief outline, or both will be included. If illustrations are to be an important element, that should be mentioned in the proposal, along with the author's ideas for them—photographs, drawings, etc.

Since the editor usually knows the author's work and reputation, the proposal will be enough for him to decide whether or not the project seems right for his list. If his decision is "yes," the established author—like the beginner—will then move on to the research stage.

3

Researching, Outlining, and Writing a Juvenile Nonfiction Book

E ACH BOOK DEMANDS its own research approach, and you have to discover it as you go along. With most subjects, a good library will be your first stop. You should begin with the card catalogue and look first for your main subject heading. For example, when I was researching *Chimney Sweeps*, I naturally turned to "Chimney Sweeps and Sweeping" and jotted down all the relevant titles and their call numbers. But I didn't stop there. Realizing that I would need to know the history of chimneys and their development, I looked up "Chimneys" next. And since chimney sweeping was an early and glaring example of child labor, I turned to that subject heading also. By the time I was finished, I had begun to build a sizable bibliography.

As you assemble your bibliography, it's a good idea to emphasize primary sources—first-person accounts by people who were present at a particular event: letters, diaries, or historical documents like the Parliamentary investigations into the living and working conditions of British climbing boys that I found for *Chimney Sweeps*.

A particularly good example of the use of primary source material is Jim Murphy's prize-winning book *The Boys' War*. It draws on letters and diaries written by Union and Confederate soldiers to give readers a vivid, firsthand picture of what it was like to fight in the Civil War.

But sometimes no "I was there" material is available, and you'll have to rely on secondary sources: articles and books written long after the fact. Then you'll need to keep your antennae up in order to catch those windy generalities that so often mask a lack of knowledge, or the inclusion of statistics and other historical data that, for one reason or another, arouse your suspicions.

In doing research I—along with most juvenile nonfiction authors—feel a special responsibility to my young readers, for I know that my book may be the first they will have read on the subject. Consequently, I try to check each fact against at least two other sources before including it in the text. Such double- and triple-checking can turn up myths that have long passed as truths. For instance, while researching *Fireworks, Picnics, and Flags*, I read two books that said an old bell-ringer sat in the tower of Independence Hall almost all day on July 4, 1776. He was waiting for word that independence had been declared so that he could ring the Liberty Bell.

At last, in late afternoon, a small boy ran up the steps

of the tower and shouted, "Ring, Grandfather! Ring for Liberty!" The old man did so at once, letting all of Philadelphia know that America was no longer a British colony. It makes a fine story; however, according to the third source I checked, it's apocryphal and appeared for the first time in a mid-nineteenth century textbook titled *Myths and Legends of the Revolution*. Knowing that, I still included it in my book—but I presented it as a good yarn, not a true story.

One of the best ways to immerse yourself in the background of your subject, whether it be historical or contemporary, is to visit the sites where the events took place. For *Fireworks, Picnics, and Flags*, I spent two days at Independence National Historical Park in Philadelphia, toured Independence Hall, visited the rented rooms nearby where Thomas Jefferson drafted the Declaration of Independence, and watched a group of awed third-graders touch the Liberty Bell in its pavilion. All of these experiences enabled me to infuse the text with lively, firsthand details that I couldn't have obtained from any book or article.

Russell Freedman is a great believer in on-site research. In his Newbery acceptance speech for *Lincoln*, he said: "There's something magic about being able to lay your eyes on the real thing—something you can't get from your reading alone. As I sat at my desk in New York City and described Lincoln's arrival in New Salem, Illinois, at the age of 22, I could picture the scene in my mind's eye because I had walked down those same dusty lanes, where cattle still graze behind split-rail fences and geese flap about underfoot."

Personal interviews are another way of enlivening your nonfiction book with unique, firsthand material. They can help make a complex scientific subject clear and exciting for your readers, as did Caroline Arnold's interviews with paleontologists at the Los Angeles Page Museum in preparation for her photo essay, *Trapped in Tar: Fossils from the Ice Age*. Or they can give you a better perspective on recent developments in a particular field, which was the upshot of my interview with the head of the Milk Safety Branch of the Department of Agriculture when I was researching *Milk: The Fight for Purity*.

Most authors today use small, unobtrusive tape recorders when doing interviews. But I, like some other writers, still prefer to take notes by hand in a pocket notebook. I find this method gives me a better chance to clarify points as the interview progresses, and to jot down only what seems significant, whereas, in editing transcribed tapes, I've often felt as if I were plowing through a mound of useless material before I came to any gems.

Whenever I go out on a research expedition, whether it's to a library or an actual site, I always take along a supply of ruled $4'' \times 6''$ cards. At the top I write the subject for handy reference later when I file the cards alphabetically in a metal box. I also write the title, author, publisher, and date of the book I'm reading so that I'll have all that information on hand when I compile the bibliography and source notes for the book.

By no means will all of the facts I take down appear in the finished book. Only a small part of any author's research shows up in the final manuscript. But I think a reader can feel the presence of the rest beneath the surface, lending substance and authority to the writing.

Many juvenile nonfiction books contain special sections at the back, and it's good to decide on these at the research stage and begin assembling the necessary information. For example, in *Walls: Defenses Throughout History*, I decided early on that a glossary of unfamiliar terms would be helpful, so whenever I came across a new term or word, I jotted down the definition. When the manuscript of the book was finished, I put all the definitions together in alphabetical order for the glossary.

Teachers and others working with children appreciate such extensions of a book's basic text. Including William Blake's poem, "The Chimney Sweeper," at the end of *Chimney Sweeps* drew praise, and a librarian told me that a favorite feature in *The Skyscraper Book* was the section at the back entitled, "Fabulous Facts about Famous Skyscrapers," which is a listing of hard-to-believe statistics about the Empire State Building, the Sears Tower, and other lofty structures.

Added information like this can even be worked into a nonfiction picture book. For instance, of the 48 pages in Betsy Maestro's *The Story of the Statue of Liberty*, illustrated by her husband Giulio, six are reserved at the end for a table of dates connected with the statue; its dimensions; a list of the people who helped with its construction; and notes on recent repairs to it.

I used the final pages in *George Washington: A Picture Book Biography* to tell the true story of George and the cherry tree, describe the Washington Monument, and take readers on a brief tour of Mount Vernon. In this way, I avoided interrupting the flow of the main text with side issues while providing teachers, parents, and interested young readers with additional material on Washington and his times.

So keep the possibility of "extras" such as these in mind as you proceed with the research for your book, whether it be a highly distilled picture book text or a full-scale study for young adults. They can give the book added depth and help it to stand out above the competition.

Another feature that almost all juvenile nonfiction books should include is an index, but it can be compiled only after the book has been set in type and put into pages. And, since indexing requires special skills, it is often done by a professional indexer rather than the author. In any case, it's not something you'll have to be concerned about as you research and write your manuscript.

The special requirements of biographies

There was a time not so long ago when it was hard to tell what was true and what was false in many juvenile biographies. The books were filled with unsubstantiated passages of dialogue, emphasized the subjects' youthful years, and ignored the more painful aspects of their lives. For example, the highly regarded picture book biography of George Washington by Ingri and Parin D'Aulaire glossed over the fact that Washington was a slaveowner, and their biography of Abraham Lincoln ended before his assassination.

The texts of biographies for older children tended to be wordy, and only a few pages were devoted to illustrations. These were generally undistinguished line drawings or poorly reproduced photographs. Some older level biographies contained indexes, but almost none included extensive bibliographies or source notes. The reader had to go on faith alone when it came to judging the author's reliability.

Today all this has changed. School and public librarians—the most important customers for hardcover children's biographies—will no longer tolerate fictionalized dialogue in the books, and they prefer to have all quotations documented, either in footnotes or in a list of sources at the back. They fault biographies, even picture book treatments for young children, that don't offer full-scale portraits of their subjects. And they expect biographies for all age groups to be well-designed and illustrated.

What methods can authors of juvenile biographies employ in order to deal with these requirements? Here are a few suggestions:

1. Include incidents from the subject's childhood and youth with which young readers can identify, but concentrate on the adult accomplishments that make the person worthy of anyone's attention.

2. Avoid the temptation to invent dialogue and use instead extracts from letters, speeches, recollections, and other documents to bring the subject to life. Remember to make a note of where you found each quotation so that you can put this information in your source notes.

3. Don't be afraid to discuss the blemishes on the subject's personality and character. They'll make his or her virtues stand out more sharply by contrast, and result in a convincing, three-dimensional portrait. For example, in his biography *Franklin Delano Roosevelt,* Russell Freedman acknowledges the existence of Lucy Mercer, Roosevelt's longtime mistress, without dwelling on that side of the President's life.

The latter points up one of the main differences between juvenile and adult biographies. Instead of emphasizing the subject's failings, as do many adult biographers, the children's biographer admits the person's faults but accentuates his or her positive qualities.

4. Write the text fully and with a sense of the dra-

matic, but keep it as succinct as possible so that there'll be room for plenty of illustrations. And be prepared to research and gather these as part of your contractual obligations.

Picture research

Unless you're working with a photographer on a photo essay, you'll probably be asked to provide any photographic illustrations that are needed for your nonfiction book. The publisher may agree to pay part of the cost of prints and permissions, but don't count on it. (Photographic illustrations can include reproductions of historic cartoons, posters, and drawings and paintings from museums, but not original drawings or maps; the latter are usually the publisher's responsibility.)

Doing picture research is a little like playing detective. Both involve a combination of intuition and logic, with a bit of luck thrown in for good measure. I begin by making up a list of the illustrations I'd ideally like to have for each chapter in the book and then making a matching list of likely sources. After that the search begins.

Following this procedure with *Milk: The Fight for Purity*, I went first to the Metropolitan Museum and The New York Public Library, where I found evocative paintings of medieval herdsmen with cows and amusing cartoons of eighteenth-century milksellers. At the Library of Congress in Washington, I located vivid drawings of conditions in the distillery dairies of the 1850s. And the Committee for a Sane Nuclear Policy provided haunting photographs of youngsters taking part in the anti-nuclear demonstrations of the early 1960s. As with the text research, I gathered more photos than could be used in the book, but it's always better to have too many illustrations to choose from than too few.

Assembling the illustrations of *Milk* and my other books has taught me several important things about doing picture research. The first is: Never start with the well-known photographic agencies. They charge high reproduction fees which are likely to put you in the red if your contract states, as many do, that you are responsible for paying all or most of the fees.

Instead, try to think of other possible sources, such as federal or state agencies that supply photographs for the cost of the prints; or art and natural history museums, which charge modest fees; or national tourist offices, which are usually glad to give you photographs free of charge, asking only that you credit them as the source.

Manufacturers of various products are also good sources of free photos. Their public relations departments will be happy to send you photographs of everything from tractors to inflatable vinyl scarecrows in return for an acknowledgement in your book.

Wherever you obtain the photos, though, be sure they're of the highest possible quality. There's no point in submitting pictures to your publisher that are scratched, faded, or poorly composed, because he simply won't be able to use them. The only exception to this rule would be rare or historical photographs, as was the case with some of the 19th-century illustrations for *Milk*.

Outlining and writing

Once the bulk of the text research is complete and while you're still working on the picture research, you can begin the actual writing of the book. When I reach this stage, I generally draft a rough outline of the entire book, divided into chapters. I do this entirely from memory, without looking at any of the research cards in the file box. In this way, I can sum up what all the notes, assembled during a year or more of research, have meant to me, and start to give the material my own shape and direction.

Next, I carefully reread all the cards and do a more detailed outline of the book. After that, I outline Chapter One and begin writing the text longhand in a ruled, college-style notebook. Actually, I use three notebooks. One is for outlining, another for the main thrust of the writing, and when a passage gets so messy that I can't read it, I have a third notebook for my revision inserts. I type the manuscript only at the last stage and do some final polishing as I type it.

Achieving a consistent personal voice in a nonfiction book takes me at least three drafts. In the first, I get down the basic material of the paragraph or section. In the second, I make certain the organization is logical and interesting, and smooth out any spots where the style of the original research source is too much in evidence. There's always a danger in writing nonfiction that the text may be lumpy. In the third draft, I polish the section until the tone and voice are entirely mine.

I'm often asked if I think of the child reader while I'm writing, and my answer is both "yes" and "no." Whenever I come to a new topic in the text, or the mention of an historical event such as the French Revolution or the fall of the Roman Empire, I stop and ask myself, "Will readers have enough prior knowledge of this subject?" If I think they won't, I gear my writing accordingly in an attempt to provide them with the information they will need to understand what I'm saying. At the same time, I'm careful not to talk down to readers by using oversimple language that may insult their intelligence. For I firmly believe that in nonfiction, as in other types of writing for children, it never hurts to use an occasional "hard" word as long as it's appropriate. That's one of the best ways, after all, to stretch a child's—or anyone's—vocabulary.

As I'm writing, I always try to make the most of the dramatic possibilities in the material. And I deliberately employ fiction techniques of scene-setting and atmosphere-building whenever they seem valid. We'll take a look at some of these techniques in the next chapter.

4

A Nonfiction Writer Is a Storyteller

PEOPLE ARE SOMETIMES startled when I say that a nonfiction writer is a storyteller. Aren't nonfiction books and articles made up entirely of facts? Yes, of course. But the organizing and shaping of those facts into readable, interesting prose requires all the skills of a storyteller.

It begins with the idea. Since a juvenile nonfiction book often takes six months to research and another six months to write, the idea should be one that captures the writer's imagination strongly. Unless the idea has an element of story, of mystery in it, the writer may not be compelled to invest the time and energy needed to develop it.

One Christmas season I happened to see a picture of our plump, jolly Santa Claus in juxtaposition with his tall, thin ancestor, St. Nicholas. My curiosity was aroused: How did two such dissimilar figures become joined? The result was my book, *The Truth About Santa Claus*. Several years later, as I was eating dinner in a restaurant, I found myself wondering when people first began to use spoons, knives, and forks. That, in turn, led me to write *From Hand to Mouth*, which traces the story of our common eating utensils.

There's that word again: story. With each of these book ideas, I was moved to explore the story behind something, whether it was our favorite gift-bringer, or the common, everyday table fork. And it was the lure of the story, and the promise of discovering the key to it, that sustained my interest through the long hours of research.

As I do research, I'm always on the lookout for dramatic or amusing anecdotes that will help to bring the subject to life for young readers. For example, when I was researching *From Hand to Mouth* I was delighted to find the following anecdote, which tells how table knives came to be rounded.

The design of table knives changed even more noticeably in the 17th century. Now that people throughout Europe were eating with forks, they no longer needed knives with sharp points to spear their food. Consequently, by the end of the century most European table knives were made with rounded ends.

Some say Cardinal Richelieu, a French religious and political leader, was responsible for this change in knife design. The Cardinal frequently entertained a nobleman who was in the habit of picking his teeth with the point of his knife. Disgusted with the man's behavior, the Cardinal had the points of all his table knives ground down, and others in the French court followed the Cardinal's lead.

As the research begins to take shape, I frequently discover an overall narrative line in the material and build the structure of the book around it. The book *Walls: Defenses Throughout History* began as simply an account of fascinating walls I'd seen, among them Hadrian's Wall and the Great Wall of China. But it grew first into a history of fortifications and then into a demonstration that no defensive wall, from the Great Wall to the Maginot Line, has ever really worked.

From Hand to Mouth assumed a circular pattern. It opens on a scene of ancient people eating with their fingers and ends with people once again relying on their fingers in today's fast-food establishments. In between we get glimpses of all the elaborate table manners that came into being with the use of knives, spoons, forks, and chopsticks.

Neither of these patterns—these narrative lines— was imposed on the books in question. They emerged naturally the deeper I got into the research and the more connections I saw between the various aspects of the topic and the way they had changed over time. When critics talk of an informational book being well-organized, I think what they're really referring to is a sense of inner-connectedness and thematic progression. It's as crucial to the success of a nonfiction book, I feel, as a strong plot is to a novel.

Once the overall direction has been determined, the outline can be divided into chapters. Here pace is terribly important. Often what I originally thought would be one chapter contains too much information and works better if it is divided into two. Ideally, I aim for no more than ten typewritten pages per chapter, and preferably seven or eight. Most of my books for eight-to-twelve-year-olds have run to eight or ten chapters, resulting in final manuscripts of fifty to ninety pages. That length allows room for illustrations and doesn't seem too formidable to today's young readers, who are confronted with so many different media claims on their attention.

Chapter titles provide another way to inject humor and drama into a book and encourage a youngster to continue reading. Sometimes a straightforward, factual title, such as "Walls of World War II" (used in my book *Walls*) works best. But in other cases, a more dramatic approach seems called for, like "Danger from the Sky," the title of the chapter on the effects of atomic radiation in *Milk: The Fight for Purity.* Never miss a chance for humor, either, if it's appropriate to the subject, as in the chapter about European table manners before the introduction of forks in *From Hand to Mouth.* I called it "Don't Put Your Whole Hand in the Pot!"

The opening paragraphs of each chapter—and especially the first chapter—should be as intriguing as you can make them, for they may well determine whether the reader will go any farther in the book. Try not to begin a chapter with a flat, factual statement, but start instead with an anecdote or scene that will help establish the mood and draw the reader in.

For example, the opening of *The Riddle of the Rosetta Stone* might have begun with a simple statement of fact: "The Rosetta Stone played a vital role in helping us understand the literature, politics, and social organization of ancient Egypt." Instead I decided to try to interest youngsters by leading them up to the Stone in its museum setting today. Here is how Chapter One begins:

The place: The Egyptian Sculpture Gallery of the British Museum in London. The time: Now.
Near the entrance to the long, high-ceilinged room stand

two magnificent granite statues of Pharaoh Amenophis III, who ruled Egypt about 1400 B.C. Farther on is a colossal head of Pharaoh Ramesses II dating back to 1250 B.C. And beyond it, resting on a simple base, is a slab of black basalt, a volcanic rock.

Next to the statues and the head, the slab seems unimpressive at first glance. It is roughly the size of a tabletop—three feet nine inches long, two feet four and a half inches wide, and eleven inches thick. But many experts would say that this rather small piece of rock was more valuable than any of the larger objects in the room. For it is the famed Rosetta Stone, which gave nineteenth-century scholars their first key to the secrets of ancient Egypt.

I try to achieve a similar dramatic effect with all of my chapter openings but I don't always succeed. If, as is sometimes the case, the material resists dramatization, it's better not to force the issue, but to settle for a more direct, straightforward opening. Opportunities for drama are bound to come up later in the chapter.

Whenever possible, I like to include information about the contributions of non-Western peoples to the subject under discussion. This adds a multicultural dimension to the book—something all teachers and children's librarians are actively seeking today. *From Hand to Mouth*, for example, features a chapter on chopsticks and how to use them, and I've heard that this chapter has led to classroom exercises in schools from California to New Jersey.

Several other books of mine contain multicultural material. *Let There Be Light: A Book About Windows* describes the unusual ways people have found to bring light and air into their dwellings in Africa, the Middle East, and Asia, as well as in Europe and America. *Be Seated: A Book About Chairs* has a chapter on the elaborately carved ceremonial stools and chairs found in many West African nations. And in *The Truth About Unicorns*, along with an account of the traditional European unicorn, there is a description of the very different Chinese unicorn—the gentle *ki-lin* which embodies Buddhist ideals.

If you can extend your nonfiction books in similar multicultural directions, you'll provide youngsters with a richer reading experience. You'll also enhance the books' chances of being used in the classroom and in multicultural library programs.

While most reviewers and librarians are opposed to the use of invented dialogue in juvenile nonfiction, a writer of informational books can almost always enliven the text with well-chosen quotations and extracts from actual conversations. These can be humorous, like the precepts from Erasmus's 16th-century book on manners, titled *On Civility in Children*, that I quoted in *From Hand to Mouth*. Here are a few examples: "Take the first piece of meat or fish that you touch, and don't poke around in the pot for a bigger one." "Don't pick your nose when eating and then reach for more food." "Don't throw bones you have chewed back in the pot. Put them on the table or toss them on the floor."

Or the quotations can be impassioned, like the words of Nathan Straus, the New York philanthropist who led a 20-year battle to make pasteurization compulsory in the United States. In *Milk*, I quoted the following extract from a telegram that Straus sent to the Chicago Board of Aldermen:

> The pasteurization ordinance for which you are fighting means lives of babies saved; its defeat means babies killed. Can Chicago hesitate between these alternatives?

Often a quotation will contain several relevant sentences but be too long and complicated to hold the interest of young readers. In such cases, it is perfectly permissible to shorten the quotes, as long as all omitted words are shown by dots (. . .).

Are permissions required for the use of such quotations? Not if the speaker quoted lived long ago, like Erasmus or Nathan Straus. Permission is usually not required for the use of quotations by contemporary figures, either, especially if they're a matter of public record in a newspaper or magazine, and are less than 150 words. As for quotations that come from personal interviews, it's simple courtesy to offer to show the person how you've worked his material into your text. This will also serve to forestall any later claims that the person was misquoted.

Crucial as the chapter opening is in getting a reader into the chapter, the ending is equally so in summing up its content and pointing the way toward the next chapter. A novelist often plants a dramatic hook or question in the last paragraph of a chapter, and so do many nonfiction writers.

The hook can be designed to pique the reader's curiosity, like this chapter ending in *From Hand to Mouth:* "The Industrial Revolution, which started in England in the late 1700s, would spur the growth of mass production, including the manufacture of table utensils. And the people of a new nation, the United States of America, would develop their own unique way of using those utensils."

Or the hook can generate suspense, like the concluding paragraph of the chapter on atomic radiation in *Milk:* "People throughout the world aren't likely to forget the alarm they felt in the 1950s and 1960s when they first realized how easily our environment—and one of our most basic foods—can be poisoned. Meanwhile, new threats to milk have made their appearance in the 1970s and 1980s. This time they haven't come from the sky, but from right here on earth."

There's only one thing no climactic chapter hook should ever do: promise something the following chapter doesn't deliver. That isn't playing fair with the reader.

The narrative techniques I've described so far—the overall direction of the book, careful pacing, lively quotations and anecdotes, effective chapter openings and closings—all build, of course, toward the last chapter.

In fiction, this chapter contains the climax of the story and the resolution of its major conflicts. So does the concluding chapter of a nonfiction book, but instead of tying up the plot it usually features a summary of the book's content and a final statement of its theme.

This statement can have a serious tone, like the final paragraph in *George Washington:*

> George Washington left behind no children of his own. Instead he left a nation. A nation that he had served as its first Commander-in-Chief, and then as its first President. That is why he is known as the "Father of His Country."

Or the tone can be lighter, like the final sentences in *From Hand to Mouth.* (They follow a discussion of the fact that more and more Japanese today are using knives, forks, and spoons, while many Americans are trying to eat with chopsticks.)

> What's likely is that people in both East and West will continue to experiment with one another's table utensils. And who knows? Perhaps in time they will find a common

solution to that age-old problem: how to get food as swiftly, gracefully, and neatly as possible from hand to mouth.

It can even be lyrical, like the conclusion of *The Truth About Unicorns:*

> Modern science may tell us that no such animal as the unicorn could possibly exist. But we need to believe that its qualities do. Those qualities of strength and sensitivity, of courage and independence, inspired our ancestors and still have the power to inspire us. People in the future will probably be inspired by them, too, whenever they see the proud image of the unicorn.

Whichever tone seems appropriate, one element in the conclusion will always be the same, and it's as characteristic of the best nonfiction as it is of the finest fiction. This is the sense that in books, as in life, the story never really ends. Especially not in nonfiction aimed at an audience of young readers who, when they grow up, are bound to write new chapters of their own on every conceivable subject.

5

Key Elements in Juvenile Fiction: The Idea, the Characters, and the Plot

A SUCCESSFUL JUVENILE NOVEL—like a successful nonfiction book—depends first of all on a good idea. Where do authors get the ideas for their stories? In the case of writers whose work I've edited, the ideas have seemed to come from a variety of sources, but few, if any, sprang from the authors' imaginations alone.

Many ideas emerged from real-life experiences. For example, Stella Pevsner heard one day of a divorced friend whose daughter discovered she was going to have her father's new wife—whom she hadn't yet met—as her seventh-grade math teacher. How would the girl react to the woman? How would the woman treat her?

How would the girl's classmates interact with both of them? From this situation came Stella Pevsner's novel, *A Smart Kid Like You*, which was later made into the television movie titled, more explicitly, *Me and Dad's New Wife*.

Sometimes authors come across an idea for a novel while doing research for another project. Gloria Skurzynski, who writes nonfiction as well as fiction, got the idea for *Manwolf*, a historical novel for teenagers set in medieval Poland, when she was researching a medical nonfiction book and happened on the description of a rare skin disease that also causes the urine to turn red. People in the Middle Ages shunned victims of the disease and called them monsters, thus spawning the werewolf legend. Gloria imagined a boy who suffered from the disease; how would he cope with it and manage to survive? From these musings grew an unusual and powerful story.

Newspaper articles can also be an excellent source for fiction ideas. Like many other authors, Eve Bunting opens her morning paper each day with one eye cocked for a news story that might provide the basis for a novel. When she read a piece about a center in southern California devoted to the rehabilitation of injured birds, she immediately became intrigued. She arranged to visit the center, and when she saw that many teenagers worked there as volunteers, a thought occurred to her. What if one of the volunteers were a kid as much in need of rehabilitation as the birds he tended? That combination of situation and character gave Ms. Bunting the germ of her prize-winning novel, *One More Flight*.

But not all ideas lead to stories at once. Sometimes they come in fragments—a person from the author's past whom he keeps remembering and intends to work into a story someday; a dramatic situation the author wants to explore; a news story that fascinates him even though he doesn't know just how he could make use of it. If you get such ideas, don't ignore them or toss them out just because they're fragmentary. Instead, jot them down in your writing notebook or on a file card, or stick them in a folder of clippings marked "Ideas." It may be six months or five years before one of them jells in your imagination, but whenever it happens you'll have the original idea on hand to refer to.

Looking more closely at the three book ideas just discussed, you can see that a common thread runs through them. Although the ideas themselves came from different sources—personal experience, historical research, a newspaper story—they triggered a similar response in their respective authors. It's a response that all writers of juvenile fiction can use as a measure of their own ideas. First, the ideas captured the authors' imaginations and made the authors want to explore them further. Next, they envisaged dramatic situations that embodied the ideas. And finally, they imagined a central character and wondered what that girl or boy would do if confronted by the particular situation. By then, the writers had already begun to transform their ideas into stories.

Developing the characters

In shaping their stories, authors often ask which comes first, the characters or the plot. Ideally, the two should be blended closely from the start. But if you have to make a choice, you'll probably be on firmer ground if you begin with your central character.

You must know the character inside and out, psychologically as well as physically. And you must find effective ways to project your knowledge so that readers will recognize and identify strongly with the character from the moment he first appears in the story. These are not easy tasks. How can you best accomplish them?

Many successful fiction writers find it helpful to begin by putting the character in some sort of predicament. How he reacts—what he says and, more important, what he does—will not only serve to get the story started, but will also give the reader a strong first impression of the character's temperament and personality.

The predicament can be a tense one, like the crisis that engulfs fourteen-year-old Danny at the beginning of Eve Bunting's suspense story, *Someone Is Hiding on Alcatraz Island*. Danny has turned in a gang member whom he saw mugging an old woman, and now the gang is out to get him. How will Danny escape their clutches? Or it can be a predicament involving social status and prestige, as in the opening situation in *Daphne's Book*, by Mary Downing Hahn. Jessica, the heroine of this novel, is unsure of her standing with the popular girls' clique, so she naturally becomes upset when Daphne, the class outcast, is assigned as her partner in the sixth grade write-a-book project. Will she be ostracized by her "friends," Jessica wonders, if she accepts the assignment?

The predicament can even be amusing, as in Stella Pevsner's humorous story, *Me, My Goat, and My Sister's Wedding*. Doug, the hero, is secretly taking care of his best friend's pet goat while the friend is on vacation. One night the animal gets loose and frightens the neighbors when he peers into their living room window. How will Doug handle their complaints and still keep the goat hidden? (If you use a humorous situation like this in your story, don't forget one important thing: While a plight like Doug's may be funny to the reader, it usually creates a serious if not life-and-death problem for the character and should be treated accordingly. Avoid the temptation to snicker from the sidelines at the hero's dilemma; chances are you'll kill the humor if you do.)

Often, as your central character begins to take shape, a single physical or psychological characteristic will emerge as the dominant one in his personality makeup. In *Someone Is Hiding on Alcatraz Island*, Danny has to compensate for the fact that he's shorter and smaller than the gang members who are out to get him. In *Daphne's Book*, one of Jessica's chief traits is her insecurity in social situations, and it is this weakness that makes her even more reluctant to work with Daphne than she might have been otherwise. If you can find similarly dominant characteristics for your own fictional characters, you'll gain a head start in establishing their identities quickly and clearly in readers' minds.

Once you've introduced your central character and put him in a tight spot, how do you go about developing his personality—and those of the other characters—as the story progresses? The first rule to remember is that a character should be revealed much more through action than description. Although you as author need to know at the outset what your characters look like and any distinctive mannerisms they may have, you can't expect readers to be interested automatically in lengthy accounts of their pasts or detailed descriptions of their physical features.

For example, it's usually not a good idea to stop the story to describe a character: "Brian walked into the classroom. He had long black hair that fell at an angle over his forehead, and he was wearing a plaid shirt and faded jeans. The jeans were tucked into scuffed cowboy boots." Instead, try weaving the description of your character into the ongoing action of the scene: "Brian walked into the classroom late and slouched down into his seat. It didn't look as if he'd combed his long black hair, which fell over his forehead as usual. When Miss Perkins asked everybody to get ready to take some notes, Brian fumbled into the pockets of his jeans for a pencil. As he did so, his scuffed cowboy boots made a scraping sound across the floor."

In shaping their characters, some authors refer to the notebooks in which they have jotted down brief descriptions of people who have caught their eye, or possible names for characters in future stories. Names are important in helping establish the background and even the personality of fictional characters. For example, readers would no doubt expect something funny from a character named Marvin Diddlebock, whereas they might guess that a character named Liz Ashford would turn out to be the pampered daughter of a well-to-do family.

Other authors clip pictures or ads from magazines or newspapers that show people who look like the characters they have in mind for a story, and use the pictures as models while they're writing. Still others make up long lists of their characters' preferences in food, clothing, movies, books, and music. They may also think of special turns of phrase or physical mannerisms and gestures the characters would be likely to use. For example, does the hero often duck his head when asked a hard question? Does his girlfriend have the habit of twisting a strand of her hair around a finger?

Many authors base their characters on real-life prototypes, sometimes people as close to them as their own children. The advantage of this approach is that it gives them a complete, in-the-round picture of a character without their having to construct the image from scratch. But there can also be serious disadvantages: The people in question may be embarrassed or even deeply hurt when they read the story and discover they're portrayed in it. To avoid such unpleasantness, you should sufficiently alter the background and physical attributes of the characters so that the actual models won't recognize themselves. (Even then some friend or relative may think he sees himself in one of your characters.)

You may also work from the inside out—like actors who follow the Stanislavsky method—drawing on your experiences, instincts, and reactions to build a character. Of course, all characters are, to some degree, reflections of their authors' personalities, especially in stories that spring from incidents in an author's past and are largely autobiographical. However, there's a danger in relying on your own personality and feelings in book after book, for your characters may end up sounding and acting too much alike. It's usually wiser to make the characters a composite of different elements, including observation, imagination, and to some extent, real-life models, as well as your own emotions.

Point of view

While you're getting your characters firmly in mind, you'll need to make an important decision before you actually begin to write your novel. That is the point of view from which you plan to tell the story: Will it be in the third person or the first person, and will the reader see the action from the vantage point of one character or several?

In the last twenty years or so, many authors of novels for young people—especially for teenagers—have chosen to write their stories in the first person. They feel it gives the stories a liveliness and immediacy that are more likely to catch and hold the attention of readers. This may be so, but a first-person viewpoint also imposes a great many restrictions on your story. Not only will you be limited to the events and actions that your viewpoint character observes or experiences, but you'll also have to work within the bounds of *his* intelligence and perception. The result is likely to be a story that's long on one-syllable words and slang, and short on the original turns of phrase and vivid descriptive passages that make for memorable fiction.

If an author is in doubt as to which point of view to choose—first person or third person—I always recommend third. It may be more difficult to manage because of the need to stand back and account for the actions and reactions of every character in the story, but it also allows for a great deal more flexibility. You'll be able to move in and out of the characters' thoughts as necessary, but at the same time be free to describe the shifting scenes from your own point of view as author.

Some authors of juvenile fiction have experimented with telling the story from multiple points of view. For example, if the novel is a teenage romance, the author may present the various stages of its development from the girl's point of view and then the boy's. This technique can result in some dramatic and amusing contrasts, but it can also end up being repetitive and confusing. I generally find that a single viewpoint works better in most juvenile novels, especially those written for younger children.

Plotting the story

Once you've settled on the point of view, you can go on to construct the overall plot of your novel. What exactly is a plot? Basically, it is the plan or blueprint for the story, the path it will follow from beginning to end. And it's generally triggered by the steps the hero takes to resolve the predicament he finds himself in at the outset.

Every textbook on writing states that in order to have a strong plot, you need conflict, and that conflict is generated when the hero is confronted by a powerful antagonist. That's true. But there are many different kinds of antagonists, both external and internal. In *Someone Is Hiding on Alcatraz Island* by Eve Bunting, for example, Danny is chased along the San Francisco waterfront in the first chapter by the gang members who are out to get him. The plot begins to take shape when Danny decides to try to elude his chief antagonist, the gang leader, by hopping aboard an excursion boat to Alcatraz. What he doesn't anticipate is that the gang will spot him and follow in the next boat, thus moving the plot forward. Here the conflict is largely external, although the hero, Danny, is also beset by internal doubts and fears stemming from his small stature.

In *Daphne's Book* by Mary Downing Hahn, on the other hand, the conflict is mainly internal, although the heroine, Jessica, uses external means to try to resolve it. First, she goes to her teacher and asks to be excused from working with Daphne on the write-a-book contest. When the teacher refuses, Jessica meets with Daphne but is cool and distant to the girl. By behaving in this way, Jessica hopes to signal the more popular girls that she really doesn't want to have anything to do with Daphne. Daphne surprises her, though, by turning out be an interesting person. Almost against her will, Jessica begins to care about Daphne, thereby heightening the conflict within herself and advancing the plot of the book.

The plot should be governed by the actions of the main characters, as in the two novels just discussed, and at the same time those actions should reveal new facets of the characters' personalities. How the secondary characters react to the events in the plot will serve to reveal their personalities, too. From all of these revelations will come that elusive quality that's a hallmark of all good fiction: depth.

The importance of levels

Another way to give your novel depth is to make sure that you bring to the surface all the levels of meaning and significance that are inherent in the material. An excellent example of a novel that achieves this goal is Mary Downing Hahn's *Stepping on the Cracks*, winner of the 1992 Scott O'Dell Award for historical fiction.

At the outset, *Stepping on the Cracks* seems to be a story of friendship focused on two girls: shy Margaret and headstrong Elizabeth. But then the author begins to weave in additional levels. The first involves the time and place of the story: the last year of World War II in a small Maryland town. Hahn brings the period to life with carefully chosen details.

The war hasn't seriously affected Margaret and Elizabeth, although both girls have brothers serving in the armed forces. Their chief problem is Gordy, the class bully, who constantly torments them. Deciding to turn the tables on Gordy, the girls spy on his hideout in the woods and discover the boy's secret, which leads to the story's next level.

It seems Gordy is sheltering his brother Stu, a pacifist who has deserted from the army. Now the story becomes one of moral choices: What should Margaret and Elizabeth do—keep quiet about the deserter, whom they like as a person, or expose him to the authorities?

And what about Gordy? The girls find out he isn't as tough as they thought but lives in dread of his father, an abusive alcoholic. This adds another level to the boy's characterization.

At story's end, all plot threads are not tied up neatly. Stu turns himself in, Gordy and his family move away, and Margaret suffers the loss of her brother, killed in the Battle of the Bulge. Only her friendship with Elizabeth remains unchanged, a promise of hope for the future.

Several lessons can be learned about adding levels to your own stories from studying novels like *Stepping on the Cracks*. You might begin by asking yourself some basic questions when you're thinking about the plot for a new story and shaping its structure.

1. Does the main character have more than one issue to deal with, and do these issues bring out different aspects of the character?

2. Does the plot suggest the complexities of living— namely, that one's actions can have both good and bad consequences?

3. Perhaps most important of all, is the theme an important one, like the exploration of patriotism and pacifism in *Stepping on the Cracks*? Without a meaningful theme, even a novel that's superior in other respects risks being thought trivial.

Although these questions may seem relevant only to serious novels, they can be applied with equal effect to humorous material. For all types of fiction, from stories designed purely to entertain to solemn studies of death and loss, will be more satisfying to the reader if they contain a number of different levels.

To outline or not to outline

Authors often ask me if they should outline their novels before they begin to write. There's no hard-and-fast answer to that question: It all depends on the person. Some writers say they never write an outline for fear it will lessen their interest in the material and prove to be a deterrent. For instance, Jean Karl, the author of several science fiction novels for young people, once told me that she spent as long as a year thinking about her characters and what would happen to them in the course of the novel. Then, without writing any sort of outline, she simply sat down at her typewriter and let the first draft of the story pour out. "It tells itself to me as I go along," she said.

That approach may work for you, too, but most authors I've known feel more comfortable if they have some sort of outline on paper before starting their novels. The outline may be just a few brief notes for each chapter, or a detailed listing of all the twists and turns in the plot, complete with patches of dialogue and sometimes even complete scenes. Detailed outlines of the latter sort are probably most essential when you're writing a mystery and need to make sure that all the pieces of the plot fit together neatly. With other types of stories, there's a danger that too tight an outline will result in too schematic a manuscript. As editorial readers often say in their reports, "This novel has flashes of promise, but seems rigid and predictable. You can see the author's outline too clearly."

A better outlining method for most authors would

probably be to start with the central character and sketch out a rough sequence of the major incidents in which he or she will be involved throughout the story. It's helpful to know at the outset where the chapter endings will come. And you'll definitely need to know, at least in general terms, how the story is going to end. Otherwise, how can you map out the best route to get to your destination?

Beginning authors who feel confused or unsure when they start to plot their novels often find it useful to take a juvenile book they admire and break it down into a chapter-by-chapter plot outline. By doing so, they can see in a barebones way how the author moved from one incident to another, where and how he wove in subplots and introduced important secondary characters, how he injected suspense and/or humor into the story, and how he built the narrative to a climax.

You may also find it helpful to trace the path of the central character's growth through a successful published novel. What was the character's situation at the beginning? How was his personality affected by the various events that occurred during the story? How is he different at the end from the way he was at the beginning? It's often from these differences, this pattern of growth, that the theme of a novel emerges—not imposed by the author from the outside, but arising naturally from the characters and situations in the story.

Exercises like these can help beginning writers to learn the storytelling techniques of successful authors and apply them to their own writing. They may also keep them from going off on tangents when they're planning their first novels, thus saving a great deal of time.

However you go about developing the plot of your novel, whether on paper or in your head, there are several basic elements that you should always bear in mind. They apply to all types of juvenile fiction—stories for beginning readers, longer books for the upper elementary audience, and novels for young adults.

1. Begin your story with an exciting incident. If you don't engage a reader's attention on the first page, or at the latest on the second, you'll never get it.

2. End each chapter with a development or twist that will make the reader eager to go on to the next. These endings don't have to be as melodramatic as the succession of perils that beset poor Pauline in the old-time movie serial (although I once worked with an author of adventure stories who, at the end of at least one chapter in virtually all of his books, had the hero clinging desperately by his fingers to the top of a cliff). But, whether the hero is in physical danger or brooding introspectively over a decision he must make, each chapter ending should grab the reader and leave him asking that classic question: "What's going to happen next?"

3. Be aware of pacing, and try to keep the chapters in your novel about the same length. You don't want your readers to become restless and start riffling the pages because a chapter goes on too long. On the other hand, you don't want them to feel cheated because another chapter seems too short. If a chapter turns out to be twice the length of the rest, maybe it should be divided at a dramatic point in the middle. If it's much shorter than the others—two or three manuscript pages instead of the usual eight or ten—maybe it can be added to the chapter that precedes it or to the one that follows.

4. Build the plot to a dramatic and satisfying climax. This doesn't mean that you have to tie up every loose end, answer every question that's been raised, or even bring the story to a happy ending. Life doesn't work that

way, and critics and readers are likely to be skeptical if you violate their sense of reality. However, the major issues in the story should be resolved, readers should sense that the central character has grown in some way as a result of what he's experienced, and they should feel hopeful about his future.

In my opinion, a note of hope is a vital element in all types of juvenile fiction, for all age groups. While the best novelists writing for children don't deny that life has its problems and is often painful, they generally affirm that it's worth living. That's one of the qualities that distinguishes their books from many of the novels that are written and published for adults.

6

Common Failings in Juvenile Fiction—and How to Correct Them

IF A JUVENILE FICTION author comes up with a good idea for a novel, one featuring strong characters and an unusual, involving plot, the result is almost sure to be a publishable manuscript, right? No, not always. In my years as a children's book editor, I've been distressed to read many novels by both first-time and experienced authors that fell short of their potential because the authors made one or more serious mistakes in story-telling. This chapter describes some of the most common of these failings, and suggests how they can be remedied.

1. *A dull beginning.* This problem often occurs because the chief character and his situation at the outset of the story aren't introduced in a compelling way. An

author is likely to turn off readers, for example, if he devotes the first three pages of his manuscript simply to showing a teenage girl trying to decide what to wear on the first day of her sophomore year. He needs to have her dealing with a more serious issue. It doesn't have to be a life-and-death matter; suppose she's just completed a rigorous diet and is resisting the temptation to buy a Danish in the school cafeteria? That should be enough to establish her personality and get the story moving.

2. *Too much exposition in the first chapter.* In an attempt to get the necessary exposition out of the way, many authors load their first chapters with lengthy passages detailing the background of the story, and unlikely chunks of dialogue in which the characters explain themselves and their histories. After reading one such chapter, the editor I trained with early in my publishing career decreed: "All novels should begin with Chapter Two."

She may have been overstating the case, but she did have a point. I often have reason to remember her comment when I'm editing an exposition-heavy first chapter in a novel and suggest that the author simply cut it and weave the necessary background information into the subsequent chapters, in the form of brief flashbacks. In most instances, the suggestion results in a tighter, more involving story. It may work for you, too, if you are having problems with first-chapter exposition.

3. *Weak transitions.* One of the hardest writing tasks for any author is to make smooth and interesting transitions between the scenes in his story. The transitions should give readers some clue as to when and where the next scenes are taking place so they won't be confused.

Such clues should be worked in with a minimum of words in order to maintain the pace and drive of the story.

This can be tricky. Too many authors fall victim to what has been called "the door syndrome." In an attempt to make a transition absolutely clear, they feel they have to describe every move of the characters in great detail: "After saying good-bye to Grandma, Ellie went over to the front door and slowly turned the handle. As the door swung open, she stepped through it and closed it gently behind her. Then she walked down the drive to the sidewalk and hurried along it to Linda's house where she had been invited for lunch."

Do we really need to know how Ellie opened and closed the door? Wouldn't the transition work just as well—and get us more quickly to the next scene—if it simply read: "After saying good-bye to Grandma, Ellie hurried over to Linda's house where she had been invited for lunch." That's probably how I would edit the transition if I found it in a manuscript. You should keep an eye out for similar cases of "the door syndrome" in your next novel and try to correct them before you send the manuscript to a publisher.

If you find it hard to solve the problem simply by rewriting the text, perhaps you can try another scene-shifting technique that's worked well for many authors: the use of a two-or-three-line blank space between paragraphs to denote the passing of time, or a change of locale, or both. I liken this technique to a film director cutting abruptly from one scene to another in a movie. It can help to give a novel a faster pace, and is especially effective in stories of suspense where the author may need to switch quickly from the hero, who is caught in a tight spot, to his friends, who are trying to make contact with him.

But guard against relying too heavily on space breaks. If you overuse them, your writing is likely to seem choppy and disjointed. You'll probably be better off if you solve most of your transition problems in the writing itself and employ space breaks only when you want to achieve a special effect.

4. *A lack of humor or a lack of seriousness.* Rembrandt, Shakespeare, and other great artists and writers knew something that too many juvenile novelists forget: namely, that light stands out much more vividly if it's contrasted with shadow, and vice versa. If you're writing a story centered on drugs, child abuse, teenage suicide, or some other serious problem, it's a mistake to maintain an unremittingly grim mood. Silly things can be said and done in the midst of tragic events, and often are. If you inject bits of humor into your story, you'll not only vary the mood, but in all likelihood will present a more convincing and true-to-life picture.

On the other hand, if you're writing a humorous story don't be afraid to weave some serious undertones into it. The class clown may not think life is so funny when he's by himself; the joke that breaks up everyone in the fifth grade may be extremely hurtful to the person at whom it's directed. If you show both sides of such situations, you'll amuse your readers while giving them something to think about, too.

5. *Thin characterizations.* This is one of the most frequent—and most frustrating—mistakes that authors make in fiction manuscripts. Their heroes are too heroic, the villains are too villainous, and as a result their stories seem unbelievable. To avoid such failures, it's a good idea when you're planning your story and shaping the characterizations to think of a few weaknesses that will lend credibility to your hero. For example, Tom may

be a star athlete who responds immediately to any physical demand made on him. But he may also have a tendency to act rashly before he's thought through a problem. As readers see him struggling to overcome this weakness, Tom will seem more human—and more genuinely heroic. And so will your protagonists, if you give them similar feelings to grapple with.

The reverse is true of villains. In too many stories, they have no redeeming features whatsoever and consequently it's hard to take them seriously. How many people do we know in life who are totally bad? The meanest bully may love his grandmother; the most manipulative girl in seventh grade may be a gifted artist. So give your villains a few positive qualities; chances are they'll be much more convincing to readers if you do.

Remember, too, that people who behave in evil ways are often blind to the true nature of their actions. In their eyes, they aren't doing anything wrong. That only makes them—and fictional characters like them—all the more frightening.

6. *Holes in the plot.* Our daily lives are filled with coincidences and chance meetings, but we don't like to encounter them in the plots of novels. Sid Fleischman, the well-known author of many comic stories for young readers including his Newbery Medal winner, *The Whipping Boy*, offers writers some excellent advice on how to handle this problem: If there's a hole in your plot that you can't get rid of, don't try to hide it from readers. Instead, call attention to it. For example, it's better to have a character say, "I know it's hard to believe, but I ran into so-and-so on the street today" than to have your readers *think* the happening is hard to believe.

7. *Problems with dialogue.* The misuse of dialogue is responsible for many failings in juvenile novels of all

types. Here are some examples that I often see in the first drafts of novels and try to help the authors correct through revision.

(a) *Too little dialogue in a scene.* A key to overcoming this problem lies in the classic bit of advice that writing teachers have been imparting to their students for generations: "Show, don't tell." In line with this precept, it's usually a good idea to dramatize a scene, however brief, through dialogue and action rather than sum it up in a description. The descriptive approach too often results in an undesirable flatness, as in the sample scene that follows:

> After I got permission from Mrs. Peters to go to the guidance counselor's office, I left the classroom and walked down the hall to the spot where I had told my friend Billy I'd meet him. I was standing there, trying to look as if I belonged, when who should come along but Mrs. Peters.
>
> She got mad when she saw me and asked some questions. I tried to explain what I was doing there, but she didn't really listen to me. Instead, she told me I'd have to go with her to the principal's office.

After reading such a passage, I'd probably comment in the margin, "This needs some dialogue to give it life. What questions does Mrs. Peters ask the boy? How does he try to explain why he's in the hall?" And here's how the author, in an attempt to *show* rather than *tell*, might revise the scene:

> A few minutes later I was standing in the hall, trying to look as if I belonged there, when who should come along but Mrs. Peters.
>
> She frowned when she saw me. "What are you doing

here, Chris? I thought you told me you had an appointment with the guidance counselor."

"Well, I do—I mean, I did," I tried to explain. "But you see my friend Billy's in trouble, and I said I'd meet him here before next period—"

Mrs. Peters interrupted before I could finish. "It looks as if Billy's not the only one who's in trouble," she said. "I think you'd better come along with me to the principal's office, Chris."

(b) *Too much unbroken dialogue.* Sometimes, instead of failing to dramatize a scene through dialogue, authors make the opposite mistake. They rely so heavily on dialogue alone that the reader may become confused and forget who's speaking. That's what occurs, as you'll see, in this sample exchange between two girls:

"Where would you like to go later?"

"I don't know. Maybe a movie?"

"Why not? They say that new picture about aliens from another galaxy is really exciting."

"I don't like all that science fiction stuff. I'd rather see the new Meryl Streep picture. The reviewer on Channel 7 said it was terrific."

"Oh, not Meryl Streep. She's always the same."

The dialogue per se isn't what's wrong with that scene. What it lacks is a sense of context. This can often be corrected by weaving in some narrative sentences. Such sentences will not only serve to identify the speakers, but they can also be used to deepen the characterization and advance the plot.

Here's a revision of the scene, employing the exact

same dialogue, but it shows how much more texture a few descriptive sentences can bring to it:

> "Where would you like to go later?" I asked.
>
> "I don't know," said Sandra. "Maybe a movie?"
>
> That wasn't a bad idea. I'd overheard Bruce and Jerry talking about going to the sci-fi movie at the mall tonight. Maybe we'd run into them and. . . . "Why not?" I said. "They say that new picture about aliens from another galaxy is really exciting."
>
> "I don't like all that science fiction stuff," Sandra said. "I'd rather see the new Meryl Streep picture. The reviewer on Channel 7 said it was terrific."
>
> I was pretty sure none of the guys would go to *that* picture.
>
> "Oh, not Meryl Streep," I said. "She's always the same."

Notice that in the second version of the scene the author avoided unusual verbs and used no adverbs. Too many writers feel they need to enliven their dialogue by accompanying it with a different verb every time, and following each verb with an adverb. When I read a manuscript page filled with such expressions as "he muttered darkly," "she snarled nastily," "he whispered shakily," and "she cried happily," my immediate impulse is to edit them all down to a simple "he said" and "she said." The dialogue, if it's lively and appropriate, will let the reader know how the character is saying it, and no adverb will be necessary.

(c) *Dialogue that's too "trendy."* Children and teenagers constantly latch onto new expressions and make them their own. What's "swell" for one generation is "neato" for the next and "awesome" for the one after that. Authors want to be *au courant*, but with the pace of cultural change seeming to accelerate each year, they run the risk of sounding dated if they incorporate such expressions in the dialogue of their novels. Even expressions that are right up-to-the-minute when the manuscript is written may be out of date or unknown to readers by the time the book is published two years later.

I often recall what the well-known novelist for teenagers, M. E. Kerr, replied when asked how she managed to keep the dialogue in her stories up-to-date: "I don't try," she said. "I do my best to avoid slang and jargon and rely on simple, basic words to express my characters' feelings."

As an editor, I also question the overuse of contemporary references and suggest that authors find other ways to convey their characters' preferences in movies and music. Most hardcover juvenile novels—unlike most adult novels—stay in print for at least three years, and often many more. So why fill them with references to rock groups and TV stars who may be long forgotten when the books are still finding readers?

8. *Weak entrances and exits.* Many fiction manuscripts are seriously weakened because the authors fail to provide their characters with effective entrances into key scenes and strong exits out of them. The first entrance of a main character in the story is especially important. Skillfully handled, it can establish the personality of the character in a few swift strokes. If the moment is lost, though, it may require several pages of dialogue and description to convey what a dramatic entrance would have accomplished in a couple of paragraphs.

Suppose, for example, that your heroine is a likable but clumsy girl who's invariably late and always seems to trip over her own feet. In the first draft of the story you may pass too quickly over her first entrance, as in the excerpt that follows:

> Amanda walked into the kitchen around ten on that Saturday morning, her roller skates dangling over one shoulder. "Hi, Mom," she said. "Sorry I'm late. I just couldn't seem to get myself together."
>
> "I understand, dear," Mrs. Spence said, "but I'm afraid you'll have to make your own breakfast."

There's nothing glaringly wrong with that exchange; it just isn't very interesting. And it certainly doesn't make use of Amanda's entrance to give the reader a vivid first impression of her. In an editorial note, I might ask the author if Amanda's mother is exasperated when Amanda is late for breakfast again. Does she call up to her? And what about Amanda? Does she have any problems on the stairs before we see her? After pondering these questions, here's how the author might rework the scene:

> Mrs. Spence strode over to the archway and called upstairs. "Amanda, where are you? It's nearly ten!"
>
> "Be there in a sec, Mom," Amanda called back. "I couldn't find my skates and then—" Suddenly there was a crash in the upstairs hall followed by the sound of something rolling down the steps. "Oh, oh, one of them got away."
>
> As Mrs. Spence watched, hands on hips, a roller skate clattered to a halt on the landing with Amanda right behind it. The girl's hair was a mass of tangled red curls and the tail of her blouse dangled below her sweater.
>
> "Got you!" Amanda said as she reached down to pick up the wayward skate. But in retrieving it she lost her grip on the other one. The second skate banged down the short flight of steps to the hall and was headed across it when Mrs. Spence stopped it with her toe.

A bright red blush spread across Amanda's face. "Sorry, Mom," she said.

Mrs. Spence had to smile. "Oh, Amanda, what are we going to do about you?"

In that revision, we get a much sharper picture of Amanda, and it's achieved through a lively, amusing scene that advances the story's action. Ideally, that's what every first entrance should do.

Exits can be as difficult to manage as entrances, and often more so. Sometimes I sense that authors shy away from making the most of a character's exit for fear of seeming melodramatic. But I'd much rather see an author risk a little melodrama than throw away the possibility for a strong exit, as happens in the following exchange between a father and son:

"I don't want to hear any more about it," Mr. Andrews said. "You're grounded for two weeks, Johnny, and that's that."

"All right," Johnny said. He left the living room and went up the stairs to his room.

That exit is so understated that it's virtually no exit at all. What is Johnny feeling? we wonder. Is he angry, bitter, resigned? How does he leave the room—slowly, quickly? How does he go up the stairs? Dragging his heels, hoping his father will call him back? Or in a run, wanting to get away from the man as soon as possible? In responding to those questions, the author might come up with this revision:

"I don't want to hear any more about it," Mr. Andrews said. "You're grounded for two weeks, Johnny, and that's that." He turned away then, and went to the bar to pour himself a fresh drink.

"All right," Johnny muttered under his breath, so softly that he doubted if Dad heard. Who cares? he thought to himself. Dad never hears anything I say anyway.

With a last glance at his father's back, Johnny left the room and started up the stairs. He took them one at a time, giving his father a chance to call him back if he wanted to. But he didn't; Johnny hadn't really expected that he would.

When he reached the door to his room, Johnny had a momentary impulse to slam it behind him, then decided against it. Instead he closed the door so gently that he could barely hear the latch click into place.

Fleshing out an exit in this fashion can accomplish several things at once. Here, as Johnny climbs the stairs to his room the reader gains an insight into the boy's emotions and sees how he reacts to a crisis. However, authors are sometimes reluctant to undertake such revisions. They worry that if they do, their manuscripts will get too long and seem overwritten. They should keep in mind one of the basic principles of editing—namely, that it is always easier to make cuts in a scene that goes too far than to build up a scene that doesn't go far enough.

9. *Mid-book sags.* Sometimes, as I begin to read a new fiction manuscript by one of our regular authors, a smile comes over my face. The characters and situation are interesting, the plot is moving forward at a rapid clip, dialogue and description are in just the right balance. Then I turn the page and my smile fades, for I realize that the story has suddenly sagged. It's only temporary, I hope, and I keep on reading. But now I have my editorial pencil out, ready to jot down suggestions that may help the author get his story back on track.

When I analyze the problem, I usually find that the

cause of the sag is a scene or character that doesn't advance the plot. Often an author wants to take his characters to a particular locale—say an amusement park or a county fair—because he thinks it will add color to the story; instead, it merely slows it down. Or perhaps an author will introduce a character who seemed necessary at outline stage, but who has no real part to play as the story takes shape on paper.

The latter was the cause of a serious mid-book sag in the first draft of Stella Pevsner's novel, *Cute Is a Four-Letter Word*. The heroine, Clara, lived with her divorced mother near Chicago, and the entire action of the novel took place there except for one chapter when Clara visited her father, an advertising executive in New York City. He took her sightseeing and they had several warm conversations in which they admitted that they missed each other. But none of this seemed to have any bearing on the plot of the story, which picked up only after Clara returned to Chicago.

I pointed out this sag to the author in my editorial letter; she thought about the problem for a few days, and then she called me with a possible solution. "Why don't I just kill off Dad?" she said. "I don't think I need him in the story." I agreed, and in the published book Clara's father has been dead for several years, and she makes no trip to New York.

If you hit a similar mid-book sag in one of your own novels, it's usually a good idea to go back to the original outline and ask yourself some hard questions. Does every episode and character help to move the story toward its conclusion, or are some of them extraneous? If your answer to the latter half of that question is "yes," then drastic surgery may be called for, as was the case in *Cute Is a Four-Letter Word*. Such surgery can be painful for you to perform because you may lose a favorite character or plot twist in the process. But it'll probably result in a tighter manuscript—one that will hold your readers' attention to the end.

10. *An unsatisfying ending.* Just as the beginning of a novel should draw the reader swiftly and surely into the story, so the ending should send him away satisfied and elated. I have my own test for a successful ending: Does it send tingles down my spine? In far too many instances I'm disappointed, and—sensing that young readers will be also—I try to get at the reason the ending failed to move me so that I can help the author come up with a better alternative.

Often I find that the author has spent all of his energy in building the novel to a strong climax and has then cut off the denouement too abruptly. That's what happened in the first draft of Mary Downing Hahn's *Daphne's Book*. After Jessica, the heroine, learned that her friend Daphne and her little sister Hope were living with their senile grandmother and trying to keep the woman's condition a secret, Jessica promised not to tell her mother or anyone else about their problem. But when the grandmother's condition worsened and Jessica feared what she might do to Daphne and Hope, Jessica broke her promise. In the climax, she told her mother about the situation, and her mother in turn informed a social worker. The grandmother was taken to a hospital where she soon died, and only much later did Jessica learn, via a letter from Daphne, that she and Hope were now living with a cousin in Maine.

From the climax on, this ending was a letdown. What was needed was more than just a letter from Daphne; readers would want to see the girls together one more time. So the author added a powerful new scene in which

Jessica visits Daphne and Hope at Roseland, the children's home where they're staying until their cousin can come for them. At the beginning of the scene, Daphne is still angry with Jessica for having betrayed her and her grandmother to the authorities. Jessica manages to explain herself, however, and by scene's end the girls have reached a bittersweet understanding. Their friendship is as strong as ever, but they know they'll soon be parted, perhaps forever. Here's how the novel ended:

> "Goodbye, Jessica." Daphne released my hand and turned toward Roseland. "Did you really mean what you said?" she asked suddenly, her face swinging toward me in the dusk.
>
> I nodded, knowing immediately what she meant. "Yes, you're the best friend I've ever had."
>
> "You, too," she said. Then she was gone, running toward the glowing windows of Roseland with Hope behind her, looking back and waving.

When I came to those final paragraphs in the revised manuscript, my spine was really tingling. Apparently they had the same effect on other readers, for reviewer after reviewer commented on the book's strong ending, and the author received numerous letters from young readers saying it had made them cry.

What lesson can be learned from this? Simply that readers young and old like nothing better than to have a good cry—or laugh—when they finish a book. So don't be afraid to pull out all the stops and write the ending of your novel as fully and emotionally as you can. If you go too far, your editor will bring you back to earth. But if you hit the right notes, chances are you'll arrive at an ending that your youthful readers will remember for years to come.

7

The Five Ages of Juvenile Fiction

THE BASICS OF IDEA, characterization, and plot, of skillful dialogue, humor, and strong conclusions, are common to all types of juvenile fiction. However, each age group, from easy stories for beginning readers to young adult novels, has its own specific requirements. This chapter will explore the needs of each group in turn, starting with stories aimed at children of six to nine.

Easy readers

Easy reading stories are designed for children in the early elementary grades who have graduated from picture books but aren't quite ready to tackle full-length novels. The pattern for all future easy readers was set by Harper & Row in 1957, when the firm published the first title in its "I Can Read" series, *Little Bear* by Else

Holmelund Minarik, with illustrations by Maurice Sendak. Its format resembled a regular children's novel, but the text was set in larger type than usual and the book was only 64 pages long.

By the 1970s, Harper had hundreds of "I Can Read" titles in print, and a half dozen or so other publishers had jumped on the easy-to-read bandwagon with their own series. The market for easy readers became glutted, and in recent years many series have been dropped. But Harper (now known as HarperCollins) and several other houses continue to publish them, and children in first and second grade still turn to easy readers when they're looking for "a real book."

If you think you'd like to write an easy reader, it's important to keep several basic rules in mind. First, the format of an easy reader is more rigid than that of any other type of juvenile fiction. As in *Little Bear*, there are almost always a certain number of characters in each line of type, and a certain number of lines per page. If the story is divided into chapters, there may be a desired number of text lines per chapter, and most easy-reading series have a standard length for the manuscript as a whole. Some publishers also require authors of easy readers to work from a limited list of simple words prepared by a reading expert.

Before you begin to plan your easy-reading story, let alone write it, you should obtain the particular specifications of one or more publishers of easy readers. You should also study some of the easy-reading titles you admire to see how the authors structured their stories.

Watch out, though; in mastering the *form* of the easy-reading book, too many authors neglect the *content*. They forget that no youngster will stick with a book just because it's easy. It has to be interesting, funny, or exciting—like any other type of fiction—if it's going to capture and hold his attention. So, when you're developing your easy-to-read story, don't think it has to be a gentle, whimsical tale of animal friends or a mild account of a second-grade tiff. A plethora of those were published at the height of the easy-reading vogue and probably contributed to its decline.

Concentrate instead on the same basics of idea, characters, and plot as you would for a longer novel. Don't rule out any type of story: mysteries, historical stories, and science fiction tales have all appeared in an easy-reading format, along with home-and-school stories and animal fantasies. And remember that the use of simple words and short sentences doesn't mean the writing style has to be choppy or dull. The best easy-reading stories, like Arnold Lobel's books about Frog and Toad, achieve a kind of poetry through the careful choice of words linked in a flowing, rhythmic manner. That's the effect you should aim for in your own stories.

Chapter books

The next step up from easy readers is a type of story that has become known in recent years as a chapter book. These are stories written in short chapters and directed toward seven-to-ten-year-olds. Chapter books have also been called "chewy stories," meaning ones that youngsters who have gone beyond easy readers but aren't quite ready for full-length novels, can really get their teeth into.

While the name chapter book may be new, the form is not. Maud Hart Lovelace, Carolyn Haywood, Beverly Cleary, and others were writing skillful stories in chapters for the seven-to-ten age group as far back as the 1940s, and there are earlier examples dating to the turn of the century. What *is* new is the greater emphasis publishers are putting on the category, and the wider range of opportunities it offers to authors.

Chapter books are almost always divided into chapters of five to seven manuscript pages, and the overall manuscript may run anywhere from thirty to a hundred pages, depending on the complexity of the story. Unlike easy readers, chapter books do not have to be written to any exact limitations in terms of characters per line of text or a controlled vocabulary. But most of them have a tighter focus than novels for older children.

The cast of characters is generally small, and the action takes place within a fairly short time span. In this regard, chapter books resemble long short stories or novellas more than full-length novels. Consequently, when you're thinking of writing a chapter book, you should avoid a complicated plot with subplots and look for an idea that can be expressed through a single dramatic (or comic) situation.

Chapter books, like easy readers, run the entire fictional gamut from realistic stories such as Jane Resh Thomas's moving account of a farm boy and his fearful pup, *The Comeback Dog*, to Stephen Manes's broad farce, *Be a Perfect Person in Just Three Days*. Although the manuscripts are short, multi-leveled relationships can still be explored, as in Carla Stevens's *Anna, Grandpa, and the Big Storm*, and strong feelings expressed, as in Sue Alexander's *Lila on the Landing*. The genre also embraces historical fiction, the most notable example of which is undoubtedly Patricia MacLachlan's Newbery Medal-winning story of two frontier children and their father's mail-order bride, *Sarah, Plain and Tall*.

The chapter book is no longer limited to seven-to-ten-year-olds, either. In recent years, as the trend in children's fiction has been toward shorter manuscripts, many authors of novels for upper-elementary-grade readers and even some for young adults have employed the small cast and close focus of the chapter book in their more mature books. So if you have an idea for a small-scale work, don't dismiss it out of hand as suitable only for short story treatment. Examine it carefully to see if it might be shaped into a chapter book.

Middle-grade fiction

The phrase "middle-grade fiction" has nothing to do with its quality. It refers to fiction written for children in the middle elementary grades—probably the largest single audience for children's book writers. Why is this so? Because children eight to twelve are old enough to enjoy reading and can handle full-length novels, but are still young enough to want books written especially for them. After they reach the age of twelve or so, many readers—especially the better ones—move on to adult books.

Fiction aimed at this age group is dominated by contemporary home-and-school stories, although publishers' catalogues also include a considerable number of mystery, fantasy, and historical novels for eight-to-twelve-year-olds. The requirements for the latter three categories will be taken up in the next chapter; as for stories with home and school settings, they usually rely more on dialogue than on description and move at a fairly rapid clip. In editing them, I often suggest that authors divide longer paragraphs in two for ease of reading and a faster pace. Most chapters in middle-grade novels run to ten or twelve manuscript pages, and few manuscripts are more than 150 pages long.

Following the longstanding precept that youngsters like to read about children who are a little older than themselves, most of the protagonists in middle-grade fiction are twelve or thirteen. The problems confronting these heroes and heroines cover a broad spectrum. They range from worries about a seventh-grade prom, as in Eve Bunting's *Janet Hamm Needs a Date for the Dance*, to coping emotionally with the death of a best friend, as in Katherine Paterson's Newbery Medal-winning *Bridge to Terabithia*.

Some authors, when planning a novel for middle-grade readers, decide to extend their idea and plot into a whole series of stories about the central character or characters. This is understandable, given the popularity of such longstanding series stars as Nancy Drew and the Hardy Boys, and more recent characters like Beverly Cleary's Ramona, Lois Lowry's Anastasia Krupnik, and the preteen cast of Ann Martin's phenomenally successful Babysitters' Club series. But it usually proves to be a risky practice. In most cases, authors would be well advised to wait until young readers respond strongly to a character before writing more stories about him. Meanwhile, they can concentrate their energies on making the first story about that character as salable as possible.

Lively, well-written novels for upper elementary age readers have been in demand ever since publishers began to issue separate lists of children's books in the early 1920s. If you have a feeling for this age group and can think of story ideas that would appeal to it, you stand a very good chance of finding a publisher for your manuscript—and an enthusiastic audience of young readers.

Transitional novels for teens

Although the term has been in use for many years now, I sometimes wonder if there really is such a thing as a young adult novel. By the time most young adults reach the age of fifteen or sixteen, they're reading adult books exclusively. I prefer to use the term "transitional novel" because I think such stories help readers between the ages of ten and fourteen make the transition from children's to adult fiction.

Titles play an important role in attracting the attention of this age group, and authors have come up with some catchy ones in the last couple of decades. Among those that stick in the memory are Elaine Konigsburg's *From the Mixed-Up Files of Mrs. Basil E. Frankweiler*, John Donovan's *I'll Get There, It Better Be Worth the Trip*, and Paula Danziger's *The Cat Ate My Gymsuit*. Be careful, though, not to push a title idea too far and end up with one that seems forced rather than clever.

As with middle-grade fiction, most transitional novels move along at quite a rapid pace in chapters of twelve or so manuscript pages, with the total length of the book rarely exceeding 200 pages. The subjects treated in transitional novels are similar to those in middle-grade fiction, and the time periods covered range from the ancient past to the far future. However, starting in the 1960s and continuing into the early 1980s, the field often seemed to be dominated by the "problem novel."

Judy Blume pioneered the problem genre and aroused controversy with such titles as *Are You There, God? It's Me, Margaret*, which touched on Margaret's confusion about menstruation, and *Then Again, Maybe I Won't*, which confronted a boy's problems with masturbation. Other authors, including Norma Klein, Richard Peck, John Donovan, and R. R. Knudson followed in Judy

Blume's wake with problem stories of their own. By the 1970s there was virtually no topic, from drug addiction to child abuse to homosexuality, that hadn't been explored in at least one transitional novel for young teens. With the 1980s came an inevitable counter-reaction. Conservative groups launched campaigns to have books they considered "indecent and immoral" removed from school and public libraries, and many of the titles they attacked were teenage problem novels. At the same time, young readers themselves, reflecting the mood of the country, began to lose interest in problem stories and expressed a preference for light, romantic fiction. Authors and publishers responded with series after series of romance novels, most of which appeared in a paperback format.

More recently, series of horror stories by writers like R. L. Stine have attracted a large audience of young teens. These series were no doubt inspired by the popularity of Stephen King's and Dean Koontz's adult horror novels with teenage readers.

In light of such swings in audience reaction, I usually advise authors who approach me with an idea for a problem novel to put the characters and plot, not the problem, in first place. The day when any subject, in and of itself, was enough to generate reader interest is long over. If the characters in a novel aren't convincing and the plot compelling, hardcover editors aren't likely to give the manuscript serious consideration, no matter how timely and urgent a problem it explores.

The same is true of teenage romance novels: They have to contain more than just romance in order to justify the high price of a hardcover book. As for paperback publication, a certain "Hollywoodization" seems to have occurred in the romance field in recent years. More and more paperback editors appear to be relying on series stories which, like the scripts for a television series, are generally written on assignment by established professionals. Consequently, it's become more difficult for a newcomer to break into the paperback romance field.

Nor are romances as easy to write as many authors think. To bring one off successfully, you must care as passionately as your heroine about clothes, hair, the state of her complexion, and whether or not the handsome new boy in school will look her way. In this connection, I'm reminded of a conversation I once had with Jane Claypool Miner, author of many popular teenage romances. When I asked her how she achieved the enthusiastic tone of her books, she said, "I was a very romantic teenager myself—I loved to go shopping and try out new make-up and hair styles. In fact, I still do. So I just draw on all that when I'm creating my characters, and I guess it must get across to my readers." I have a hunch that this kind of empathy is a prerequisite for all writers of romance novels.

Horror stories present a different set of problems for the writer. How can one achieve the necessary chills and suspense without resorting to the mindless bloodletting found in so many contemporary movies and television programs?

One way is to describe a violent act by implication rather than spell out every gory detail. Alfred Hitchcock made skillful use of this technique in many of his films. If he was telling the story of an axe-murderer, he could fill the viewer with a sense of dread and shock without ever showing the axe falling or blood flowing.

Above all, don't surrender your own values and inherent good taste to what you may perceive to be the demands of the marketplace. Even if you're writing a horror novel to the specifications of a teen paperback series, what's to prevent you from writing it as well as you are able and developing the characters in depth? No doubt your editor will appreciate the smooth, satisfying way you've managed to tell your story. So will your readers, although they may not articulate it. And you can take an honest pride in your work instead of feeling cynical about it.

Fiction for young adults

Returning to the hardcover area, let's take a quick look at that increasingly rare breed, the novel written especially for adolescents of fourteen and up. In the face of competition from adult books, a novel for young adults has to be truly outstanding in its plot, characterization, and writing style to get favorable reviews, win acceptance by librarians, and attract a wide audience of teenage readers. Often the only things that distinguish this type of novel from its adult counterparts are a shorter length and the fact that it almost always centers on a teenage protagonist. If the story includes sex scenes, they're generally less graphic than those in an adult novel. Profanity in dialogue is kept to a minimum. And the endings of most novels for young adults, like the endings of stories for younger children, are realistic but hopeful.

Among the recent novels that have met these criteria and won a lasting place in the hearts of teenage readers are *The Pigman* by Paul Zindel, *Gentlehands* and *Night Kites* by M. E. Kerr, *Hatchet* by Gary Paulsen, and *The Chocolate War* by Robert Cormier. If you're interested in writing serious fiction for young adults, these books are well worth studying in terms of scope and craft. However, if you're in any doubt about which age group to write for—the transitional ten-to-fourteen-year-old group or young adult readers of fourteen and up—I'd give you the same advice I've given to many fiction writers: go younger. The audience for your book will probably be larger, their response more gratifying.

8

Mystery,
Historical Fiction,
Multicultural Fiction,
and Fantasy

WITHIN EACH AGE GROUP, from the "easy reading" category to novels for young adults, several different types of fiction frequently appear. The most common of these types are mysteries, historical stories, fantasies, including science fiction, and a more recent but fast-growing category: multicultural fiction. Let's look now at some of the special requirements for each type, starting with mysteries.

Mystery stories

Back in the early 1960s, many juvenile mysteries still

fell into what some critics called the "Who buried the family jewels in the backyard?" category. A brother and sister, often named Johnny and Janie, visited Great-Aunt Louisa's farm for the summer, and while there discovered a priceless heirloom that an ancestor had buried in the back garden for safekeeping during the Civil War.

Mystery stories like this were immensely popular in the 1940s and 1950s, and some are still being submitted for possible publication. Few are accepted, however, since readers now want their mysteries to have a contemporary feel. For younger children, that often means stories about a bunch of bright, perky kids who solve a neighborhood mystery. The setting is usually suburban—after all, how many children today have a Great-Aunt Louisa who lives on a farm?—and the tone is light and laced with humor. Entertaining examples of this type of mystery, for children seven to ten or so, have been written by Susan Meyers, Dorothy Haas, and E. W. Hildick.

Successful mysteries for middle-grade readers have a sharper edge than their counterparts in the past and often center on a contemporary problem such as drugs or shoplifting. A good example of this trend is Barbara Holland's suspense story about a kidnapping, *Prisoners at the Kitchen Table,* in which a wealthy young girl and her friend, a cautious boy, are held for ransom by a husband-and-wife team and must find a way to escape from their captors. Similar stories of suspense, such as those written by Joan Lowery Nixon, are popular with readers ten and up.

In *plotting* a mystery for any age group, you should keep in mind certain basic questions that will have to be answered during the course of the story:

1. What really happened? You'll need to know this before you start writing so that you can place clues logically and dramatically along the way.

2. Who is the detective, and why does he or she want to solve the mystery? What's at stake? Even in a light-hearted mystery for younger readers, the stake should be something important—at least to the central character. Finding a missing glove probably wouldn't be enough to sustain a story, but finding a missing bicycle might be.

3. What's the detective's plan of action for solving the mystery? What active steps does he take? From these the plot will naturally grow.

4. What's the opposition? Who's out to stop the central character from solving the mystery—and why? The conflict in the story will spring from your answers to these questions.

5. What's the time limit? If the central character has only a few days or a week to solve the mystery, tension will be heightened. This time limit doesn't have to involve anything as dramatic as a bomb going off. In Dorothy Haas's *To Catch a Crook*, the limit is just a deadline for a Career Day project at school, but it serves the same purpose.

Juvenile mystery writers often wonder if they should include scenes that depict violence: After all, we live in a harsh world, and even young children are constantly exposed to scenes of violence on television and sometimes on the streets in their own neighborhood. Isn't it only realistic to show this in their books?

I believe that an author for children can be realistic without being overly graphic. For instance, if the young detective in a mystery story was attacked by a gang of bullies, I wouldn't encourage an author to have them burn his arms with a cigarette to get him to talk (although that might conceivably happen in real life, or in an adult mystery). However, I would accept a scene in which the gang *threatened* to do so; that would convey the reality and danger of the situation without portraying actual violence.

Some authors consider the mystery genre inferior and not deserving of their best efforts. I strongly disagree. It seems to me that in juvenile mysteries the characterization should be just as full-bodied, the plots just as convincing, and the writing style just as smooth as in other types of juvenile fiction. Why shortchange youngsters who enjoy a good mystery by giving them books that are lacking in literary value? That's no way to encourage a love of reading.

Historical fiction

Since the 1950s, historical fiction for children has experienced a series of drastic ups-and-downs. Virtually every publisher of books for children issued large numbers of historical novels in the 1950s, on subjects ranging from life in Ancient Egypt, to the experiences of cabin boys who sailed with the early navigators, to the trials and tribulations of 19th-century American families traveling westward in wagon trains.

In the late 1960s and 1970s, however, interest in history faded. There was a slow revival in the 1980s, fueled in part by the realization that what was happening in the present could not be fully understood unless a person, young or old, had some grasp on what had happened in the past. At the same time, there arose a demand for novels that dealt with earlier periods more honestly and realistically than was true previously. No longer, for example, would librarians, reviewers, parents, or children accept stories in which all the pioneers were shining heroes and all the Native Americans villains.

Further, there is now an increased emphasis on accuracy in historical fiction. Librarians and teachers are constantly on the alert for anachronisms and factual errors in the novels they evaluate, and often they will refuse to purchase a book that fails to meet their standards, even though it may have lively, three-dimensional characters and an involving plot. To avoid rejection, historical novelists must do as much research in the periods of their stories as nonfiction writers would.

Such research shouldn't be limited to the main political events of the time—wars, revolutions, etc.—but should include the most minute details of domestic life. For instance, if toothbrushes weren't known in the 12th century, you'd better not have your heroine using one in a story set during the reign of Eleanor of Aquitaine.

The dialogue shouldn't contain anachronisms, either. While you don't want to overload it with such antique language as "Gadzooks" and "By your leave, Madam," you shouldn't have your 19th-century hero saying "I've got to get my act together" or other contemporary slang expressions. You can insert a few old-fashioned words to give the dialogue a period flavor, but you should rely for the most part on the same basic, simple words you'd use in the dialogue of stories set in any era. And you should avoid dialect unless it's absolutely necessary; too often it comes across as a kind of stereotyping, and it's difficult for most readers to comprehend.

When they talk of writing historical fiction, some authors think only of stories that take place in the distant past. They forget that, for children today, something that happened ten years ago is history. The assassination of John F. Kennedy in 1963 may seem as remote to them as the assassination of Julius Caesar, and a story set in any recent period has to be researched and written with that fact in mind.

Even though Gary W. Bargar grew up in St. Louis in the 1950s, the period of his novel *Life. Is. Not. Fair.*, he read microfilms of old newspapers and magazines to refresh his memory of what was going on at the time, what TV shows were popular, and how much a tweed sports jacket cost. You'll need to do similar research if you're writing what I sometimes call a "contemporary historical novel."

But don't let yourself get too immersed in the research. While the background details of the story must be authentic, they should never overwhelm the characters and the plot, since it is these elements that will reach across time to engage the minds and emotions of present-day readers. In this regard, I recall the first reader's report at Lothrop, Lee, and Shepard on Patricia Clapp's unsolicited historical novel, *Constance: A Story of Early Plymouth*. It read: "Although all the historical details are completely convincing, it is the portrayal of the title character that makes this novel special. Constance is totally real, totally alive, and I'm sure young readers will take her to their hearts." Clearly they did, for *Constance* proved to be immensely popular, first in hardcover and later in paperback.

Remembering that reader's report, and the success of *Constance*, I always ask myself a single basic question after finishing each historical fiction manuscript that's submitted to me for consideration: "Are the central character and his problems so immediate that I forget I'm reading about a distant time and place?" If the answer is yes, then the story has succeeded both as history *and* as fiction.

You might do well to ask the same question of your own historical stories, either at the idea stage or after you've completed a first draft.

Multicultural stories

The word "multicultural" first came to the fore in the early 1990s when educators stressed the need for children's books that reflected the increasing diversity of the U.S. population. They called not only for more books about African-American and Hispanic life, but also for books that acknowledged the many recent immigrants from Asia, the Near East, Latin America, Eastern Europe, and the former Soviet Union.

Writers and publishers have responded to this call with a wide variety of novels that offer a more complete and authentic picture of the contemporary American scene. They have also made a serious attempt to correct the false impression of our first immigrants—the Native Americans—that many earlier children's novels conveyed. Now it's not likely that any writer would conceive of, or any editor purchase, a novel about the pioneer West in which the Native American characters were portrayed as evil Redskins.

The majority of multicultural novels center on African-American and Hispanic characters, but a growing number explore the Asian-American experience. Among the outstanding authors to emerge as part of the multicultural trend are Jacqueline Woodson, who sensitively depicts the feelings of adolescent African-American girls; Gary Soto, whose stories capture the imagination and vitality of young Hispanics; and Sook Nyul Choi, whose memories of the Korean War add a special poignancy to her novels about a girl caught up in that struggle.

A debate continues as to whether writers who are not members of a particular race or ethnic group have the insights and knowledge needed to portray it convincingly. Many critics assert that they do not. Others say those critics fail to give enough credit to the role imagination plays in the writing of fiction. Meanwhile, Caucasian writers such as Bruce Brooks, Mary Stolz, and Paula Fox have written successful novels featuring African-American characters. And African-American writers like Virginia Hamilton have included white characters in their books.

There are many factors to consider when approaching multicultural story material. If you're not an insider, it might be extremely difficult to bring off a story about, say, a teenage Chinese-American boy told from his point-of-view. But if you're planning a contemporary school story set in a small northern city, and aim to present a realistic picture of life in that community, you'll no doubt want to have more than a few African-American characters in the cast. Depending on the city and the immigrant groups it has attracted, you may also want to include some Hispanic, Asian-American, or Muslim characters.

Remember, too, that the word "multicultural" is not limited to people of color. Taken in a broader sense, it embraces all the many nationalities that have helped to shape the United States. So if your ancestors came from Scandinavia, and you weave some of their Christmas customs into a novel, it will be as much an example of multiculturalism as a story centered on Haitian or Vietnamese customs.

Fantasies and science fiction

If beginning writers who didn't know the range and scope of the children's book field were asked to describe a typical juvenile novel, many would probably think automatically of such classics as *Alice in Wonderland* and *Winnie the Pooh* and say "fantasy." That probably explains why so many novice authors attempt to write a fantasy as their first venture into juvenile fiction.

I've deliberately left this genre till last because, in my experience, a fantasy is the hardest type of juvenile novel to write, and also the hardest to sell to a publisher. But what about all the wonderful fantasies for children that *have* been published, you may ask. Just look at E. B. White's masterpieces, *Stuart Little* and *Charlotte's Web*, or Richard Adams's magnificent animal fantasy, *Watership Down*, or Mary Norton's delightful tale of miniature people, *The Borrowers*. Yes, look at them; then examine what makes them successful and ask yourself that most painful but necessary of questions: Do I have the talent required to write a story that will be the equal of these books? For, in the field of fantasy and its first cousin, science fiction, nothing less will do.

Let's take a look at some of the special requirements of fantasy and science fiction writing—and why they're so daunting.

1. *A high degree of imagination*, both in the conception and execution of the story. In no other fictional genre is originality so essential.

2. *The ability to create a fantasy world that's as believable and convincing as the real world.* This isn't as easy

as it may sound. For example, if you're writing a novel like *The Borrowers*, about miniature creatures, you have to make sure that everything in their world is in the proper scale. You can't have a six-inch-high man run down the path and mail a letter in a conventional mailbox. He could never reach it, let alone pull down the slot cover. Nor, at the other extreme, can you have a twelve-foot-tall giant enter an ordinary theatre and sit comfortably in a people-sized seat to watch the movie. You'll have to think carefully about every single detail in your imaginary world to make sure it's plausible on its own terms.

3. *A subtly handled theme and fully rounded characters*. Many authors of fantasies have an axe to grind or a moral point they're eager to make. A frequent theme is the contrast between our corrupt world and a more perfect one, located either in the distant past or the far future. Or the characters may find themselves caught up in a cosmic clash between the forces of good and the forces of evil; *The Wizard of Oz* is a good example of the latter situation.

The danger in trying to write such stories is that the authors may allow the moral to become too obvious and fail to pay sufficient attention to the characterizations. As a result, their heroes often seem like cardboard cutouts and the villains are equally one-dimensional. These authors forget that the theme of a fantasy, to be effective, should be subtly introduced and the characters developed with as much depth as those in any other type of novel.

4. *A compact manuscript*. I don't know why, but the manuscripts of many fantasy novels I see are at least twice as long as their realistic counterparts. It's as if the authors, once started, lose control of their imagina-

tions and end up with stories that are much too rambling and verbose. Remember, if you're planning a fantasy, that young readers of such stories have just as many other claims on their time and attention as do readers of realistic fiction.

5. *A fine literary style.* "Style" is a word that's bandied about a great deal, but what exactly do we mean by it? Webster's defines literary style as "The manner or mode of expression in language; the way of putting thoughts into words." It goes on to add a further definition: "Distinction, excellence, originality, and character in any form of artistic or literary expression: as, this author lacks *style.*"

Style is an important element in all types of writing, but it's especially important in fantasy. If you're describing the Emerald City of Oz or its equivalent, your language has to rise to the occasion. It can't seem forced, however. Nothing is more depressing than to come across an overly "poetic" description in a fantasy manuscript and sense that the author is trying terribly hard to be "stylish." It can be as painful as seeing a man or woman wearing unsuitable clothes just because they happen to be in vogue at the moment.

So, if you're writing a fantasy, be aware of the need for imaginative writing, but remember that in writing as in other activities it's always better to be yourself. Your own style—plain or ornate, direct or convoluted—will inevitably emerge and be more effective than a strained attempt at "fine writing."

The requirements for science fiction (or speculative fiction, as it's often called) are much the same as those for fantasies, with a few additions. Since science fiction stories often center on visions of future worlds, either in space or on earth, the authors need to have a firm grip on the principles of science and technology. However, the technological details must never be permitted to overwhelm the story: lengthy technical descriptions are as off-putting to readers as lengthy exposition of any kind.

After studying the above requirements, be as honest as you can about your writing abilities before you embark on a fantasy or science fiction novel. You may have loved reading such stories as a child or adult; you may consider them to be the epitome of fine children's literature. But that simply won't be enough. If you find it difficult to visualize magical kingdoms or an advanced civilization in another galaxy, or if you lack the verbal facility to bring them to life, you're likely to spend months or even years writing a manuscript that no one will want to publish. Better to survey the field—and yourself—carefully beforehand, and invest that time and energy in a different kind of novel.

9

The Wide World of Picture Books

B Y FAR THE LARGEST NUMBER of submissions that children's book publishers receive are stories intended for picture book treatment. At the publishing house where I work, for example, I'd estimate that of the five thousand or so submissions that we get in an average year, at least twenty-five hundred are texts for picture books.

These manuscripts may be one page long or fifteen, but all the authors think they can be turned into picture books. Often, the manuscripts are accompanied by a cover letter saying the author's children, or grandchildren, loved the story when it was read aloud to them. That may be true—the children probably loved the feel of Grandma's lap and the sound of her voice—but unfortunately 99% of these stories could never be published as picture books. Why? Because their authors don't understand the form and its rigid requirements.

To begin with, there are many different kinds of picture books, geared to several different age groups. Here, we'll discuss the most popular types, starting with board books for the youngest audience.

Board books

The first books toddlers six months to two years old usually see are board books—so-called because they are produced on sturdy cardboard pages that little hands can't easily tear apart.

Board books are generally only twelve to twenty-four pages long and introduce young children to the simplest of concepts: colors, sizes, shapes, basic items of clothing, etc. If they have a story line, it is minimal. The texts often consist of only one or two words per page, and the entire manuscript may not be more than fifty words.

Since the illustrations are so important in board books, many of the most popular series have been created by illustrators who are also authors, such as Dick Bruna and Helen Oxenbury. Other board books are put together by publishing entrepreneurs called packagers, who conceive of a series of six or eight titles, line up established writers and illustrators to produce them, and sell the entire package to a publisher.

Because of these practices, the board book area is one of the hardest for a new writer to break into. Before planning or writing a board book of your own, you should study published ones carefully to make sure your idea has something new and different to contribute to this crowded field. Then you should query publishers of board books to see if they'd be interested in considering your material.

Picture books for children two to five

These are sometimes described as "pure" picture books because the illustrations occupy a far greater proportion of the books than the text. But a good text is essential to the success of these books, since all picture books—no matter how heavily illustrated—depend on their texts for structure and point.

Beginning authors often make the mistake of thinking pure picture books are easy to write because the manuscripts are so short—generally no more than two or three double-spaced typewritten pages. Actually, they're as hard to do well as a poem, since each word counts and must be precisely the right one for the idea or emotion you are trying to convey.

Beginners also tend to choose clichéd plot lines for their picture book stories. Some of those editors see most frequently are: the little animal (or child) who defies his mother, runs away, gets scared by something, and learns that home is best after all; or the protagonist—animal or human—who wishes he were something else, tries several alternatives, and ends up deciding he'd rather be himself; or the child who has a marvelous nighttime adventure, only to wake and discover it was just a dream. Some writers are able to breathe new life into such overused story situations, but most authors would do well to avoid them.

The pure picture book category embraces a wide range of subject matter. Here are some of the most common types:

1. *Concept Books*. When people think of concept books for young children, alphabet and counting books usually come to mind first because they're the most prevalent. But other types of concept books are popular, too—for example, Tana Hoban's series of photographic concept books in which she encourages young readers to take a close-up look at familiar objects.

Concept books bridge the fiction and nonfiction genres, and in fact are often classified as nonfiction. Because there are so many concept books on the market—especially alphabet and counting books—they need an original idea and slant if they are to compete successfully. Mary Elting and Michael Folsom succeeded in finding such an approach in their alphabet guessing game, *Q Is for Duck*. ("Q is for duck. Why? Because a duck quacks.") Author-illustrator Catherine Stock also succeeded in her book *Alexander's Midnight Snack: A Little Elephant's ABC*. Waking up hungry at midnight, Alexander tiptoes downstairs to the kitchen where he finds the makings of a giant snack that introduce all the letters of the alphabet. What did Ms. Stock come up with for X? An X-ray showing what Alexander's stomach looked like after he'd eaten all the alphabetical foods.

If you're thinking of writing an alphabet book, you'd be well advised to put it to the X-test to see how you're going to get over that particular hurdle, which has defeated many otherwise promising alphabet book ideas. You should also ask yourself if your idea is really suited to alphabet-age youngsters of, say, three to five. Far too many authors of alphabet books use material beyond the grasp or interest of young children—*A Is for Architect*, for example. Nor do such books appeal to older children, most of whom would find them "babyish."

Story frameworks like the one in *Alexander's Mid-*

night Snack add another dimension to concept books, but they must grow naturally out of the material and not seem to be imposed on it. Whether fictional elements are introduced or not, the best concept books are carefully shaped by their authors and have strong beginnings, a mid-section that sustains interest, and usually a twist at the end to round off the book in a satisfying fashion. With structure like this, your concept book— whether it be an alphabet book, a counting book, or an introduction to colors—stands a much better chance of catching an editor's eye, and later on, the attention of children in libraries and bookstores.

2. *Animal fantasies.* Children love to read about animals and look at pictures of them. Many children also find it easier to accept the portrayal of strong emotions—anger, jealousy, etc.—if they're expressed by animals instead of children, as in Russell Hoban's muchloved stories about Frances, a little badger. The children's distance from the animals makes identification with their emotions less threatening.

Animal fantasies demand many of the same things from writers as fantasy novels. The basic idea of the story should be imaginative; the fantasy world depicted and the behavior of the animal characters within it must be believable on their own terms; the moral of the story, while clear, should never be hammered home in an obvious fashion; and the writing style should be flowing and graceful, brightened by touches of humor and lyricism.

Although the animal fantasy genre has the advantages of imagination and child appeal, it can present many pitfalls to the unwary writer. Here are several things to guard against if you're thinking of writing an animal fantasy: (a) Don't rely on cute names like Billy Beaver and Wanda Weasel for characterization. It's what the animals *do* in the story that will make them memorable, not what they're called. (b) Avoid cuteness in the dialogue, too. As for having animals talk in picture books, it all depends on what they have to say. The content of the dialogue is what's important, not the mere fact that it's an animal who is speaking.

3. *Realistic stories.* Some librarians and teachers still call realistic picture book texts "Here and Now Stories." This expression dates back to the 1930s when Lucy Sprague Mitchell of the Bank Street College of Education wrote that, along with the classic and modern fantasy tales, small children needed to have stories that reflected the here and now of their everyday world.

Author-illustrator Lois Lenski proved herself to be an early master of the realistic genre with a series of books that included *Cowboy Small.* Charlotte Zolotow has continued the tradition in such brief but probing texts as *William's Doll,* about a boy who craves a doll even though some of his friends and family think it's "sissy," and *A Tiger Called Thomas,* about another boy who overcomes his shyness when he dons a tiger costume to go trick-or-treating on Halloween.

Realistic picture books can also be a vehicle for the depiction of multicultural subjects. Black author-artist Donald Crews demonstrated this in his book *Bigmama's,* a loving evocation of summer days he spent as a boy at his grandmother's home in the South.

One of the most skilled and prolific writers of the realistic picture book today is Eve Bunting. Her stories run the gamut from the lightly humorous (*A Perfect Father's Day,* about a little girl who treats Dad to all of *her* favorite things) to intimate family dramas (*The Wednesday Surprise,* in which a granddaughter helps her immigrant grandmother learn to read) to works that explore sensitive contemporary issues like homelessness (*Fly Away Home*, which tells of a boy and his father reduced to living in a big city airport).

Editors are always on the lookout for realistic stories like these that project the child's world at home, in the neighborhood, or at school in a fresh, imaginative way. However, they receive far too many manuscripts of the "I Go to the Supermarket" variety that aren't real stories, but merely a dull description of a place or an event. Here-and-Now stories should have the same basic elements as other kinds of picture book stories: an intriguing opening, a well-developed middle, and, if possible, a clever final twist at the end.

Because the picture book form is so compressed, a writer can't afford to ramble around, as a novelist may, until he arrives at just the right ending. Knowing this, many writers of Here-and-Now stories and other types of picture books start with the climax of the story and work backward. In fact, Eve Bunting says she often writes the last paragraph of a picture book text before she writes the first.

While the subject matter in a Here-and-Now story may be mundane, the writing should never be. Without straining for effect, the story should be written in rhythmical prose and feature vivid images and turns of phrase. As in all picture books, each word is important in a Here-and-Now story. And because there are so few words on a page, they tend to jump out at the reader. Consequently, any that seem awkward or inappropriate will be much more noticeable than they would on the denser type page of a junior novel.

Besides being well-written, a Here-and-Now story should contain several different settings and other good illustration possibilities if it's to be considered seriously by a picture book editor. For example, a manuscript may have a charming tone and include many appealing, life-like touches. But if the entire action takes place in a kitchen where a mother and daughter are baking cookies, the editor will probably decide that the story has too little illustration potential to warrant picture book treatment, especially at today's high costs. The editor might suggest that the author try the story with a children's magazine, where it could be published effectively with just one or two illustrations.

Surprisingly, considering the widespread appeal of realistic picture book stories, editors receive far fewer submissions of this kind than they do in the animal fantasy and original folk and fairy tale categories. This seems a pity for, in my experience, most beginning picture book authors would stand a much better chance of selling a skillfully told Here-and-Now story.

4. *Mood pieces.* These are texts that attempt to capture the essence of an experience, a mood, in poetic language if not actual poetry. Mood pieces first came to the fore in the 1940s with the publication of such books as Alvin Tresselt's 1947 Caldecott Medal winner, *White Snow, Bright Snow* (illustrated by Roger Duvoisin), which depicts a winter snowfall and how it affects a large cast of characters.

Like *White Snow, Bright Snow*, many successful mood pieces have centered on nature themes. Tresselt himself wrote a number of them in the 1950s and 1960s, culminating in *Hide-and-Seek Fog*, which also was illustrated by Roger Duvoisin and was a Caldecott Honor Book in 1965. The latter title followed a typical mood piece pattern, opening with a scene of children playing on a Cape Cod beach on a sunny day. Then a fog rolls in, blanketing the beach and the summer houses, and the children must be content with indoor activities. At last the fog lifts, and the text comes full circle with the children back on the sunny beach on the book's last page.

Mood pieces fell somewhat out of favor in the 1970s and early 1980s, perhaps because many subjects had been treated in more than one book, and some in six or seven. After all, how many evocations of a rainy day does a library or bookstore need on its shelves? But an outstanding mood piece can still make an impact. This was demonstrated by Jane Yolen's Caldecott Medal Winner, *Owl Moon*, illustrated by John Schoenherr, which lovingly portrays a girl and her father going out in search of owls on a cold winter night.

At first glance, a mood piece may seem easy to write because there is no story line, and no need for character development. Actually, they're more difficult to bring off than other types of picture book stories, because, in the absence of a plot, the young reader's attention has to be captured and held solely by the excitement of the experience recounted and the quality of the writing. Mood pieces also require even more distinguished illustrations than some other kinds of picture books—drawings or paintings that can project the natural beauties described in the text.

Ordinariness of subject matter is the most common flaw in mood piece manuscripts. If you're thinking of writing one, begin by studying a selection of outstanding mood books in a library or bookstore to make sure you have a truly original idea. Yet another version of *A Day at the Beach*, or something similar, probably won't be considered a strong enough candidate for publication in today's highly competitive picture book market, no matter how well it's written.

5. *Retold nursery and folk tales, and picture book*

versions of songs. When you walk into the children's section of a bookstore, your eye is likely to be caught first by a display of new picture book versions of such classic nursery and folk tales as *The Little Red Hen* and *The Three Bears.* The display may also include illustrated renditions of favorite children's songs like "Roll Over" and "Papa's Going to Buy Me a Mockingbird."

Seeing books like these, many authors decide there must be a large market for retellings and hurry home to their typewriters or word processors to dash one off. Later, they're disappointed when their manuscripts come back from publisher after publisher, and they can't understand why. The answer is that almost all retellings of nursery and folk tales start with the illustrator or the publisher, not with the author. The illustrator is seeking a vehicle to display his talents, and since most such tales are in the public domain, he also sees illustrating one as a way to get the full royalty on the book instead of having to share the income with an author. If the text of the original tale needs cutting or rewriting, this is generally done by the illustrator in tandem with his editor, or sometimes by an established free lancer who is engaged for a flat fee.

In light of these realities, I usually advise authors to concentrate on original material instead of retelling a familiar tale—unless, of course, they've unearthed a wonderful old story that, for some reason, has been overlooked for generations. Even then, it's wise to check the title section of the latest edition of *Children's Books in Print,* available in most public libraries, to make sure other picture book versions of the tale don't exist.

Although you may never retell an old tale, they are still worth careful study in terms of structure as you develop your own original stories. For example, the cumulative effects that delight children in tales like *Henny Penny* and *The Gingerbread Boy* can be put to good advantage in a contemporary story. So can the pattern of threes that works so well in stories ranging from *The Three Little Pigs* and *The Three Billy Goats Gruff* to *The Three Wishes*. You may be writing about a girl who has to perform three tasks at home or school before she wins a reward instead of a prince who has to overcome three obstacles, including a fire-breathing dragon, before he wins the hand of the princess. But the classic pattern of your story is likely to be just as satisfying to young participants in a story hour today as it was to listeners gathered around a Celtic campfire 1500 years ago.

Picture story books for ages five to eight

From concept books, to retold tales, to realistic stories, picture story books cover the same broad spectrum of subjects as do pure picture books. There are only four basic differences between the two categories.

1. Picture story books are aimed at a somewhat older audience than the pure picture book—five-to-eight-year-olds instead of two-to-five-year-olds.

2. Because they're written for older children with longer attention spans, the stories may have more complex characterization and plots than those for the younger picture book set. Examples of outstanding picture story books include Vera B. Williams' *A Chair for My Mother*, Emily Arnold McCully's *Mirette on the High Wire*, William Joyce's *Dinosaur Bob*, and Joanna Cole's popular stories about the Magic School Bus.

3. Reflecting their greater complexity, texts of picture story books are longer, running from four to eight

double-spaced manuscript pages and sometimes more. As books, they may extend in length to 48 pages instead of the usual 32, and the text often takes up as much space in the book as the illustrations.

4. Whereas most of the retold tales that appear as pure picture books are animal fantasies like *The Three Little Pigs*, retellings of fairy tales such as *Rumpelstiltskin* and *Snow White* predominate in the picture story book area. As with the retellings of nursery tales, most of the new versions of fairy tales are done either by the illustrator or the editor.

There's also a limited market in the picture story book category for original tales cast in the traditional folk and fairy tale mold. Jane Yolen, for one, has made a name for herself with stories of this type including *Greyling*, *The Girl Who Loved the Wind*, and the Caldecott Honor Book, *The Emperor and the Kite*, illustrated by Ed Young. But it's a tough market for the new author to break into, since an original tale, like a fantasy novel, demands a high degree of imagination and writing skill. Most beginners would probably do better to master the craft of the realistic story before trying their hands at original tales.

Picture books for older children

There's been a surprising development in the picture book area in the last few years. No longer does the audience end with children of seven or eight. Now for some books it extends upward to the eight-to-twelve-year-old group, and even to young adults.

This development is probably due to the fact that children today are much more visually oriented than their predecessors of a generation or two ago. From infancy on, these children are used to watching hours of television every day. Consequently, picture story books with colorful illustrations no longer seem "babyish." They simply offer a different kind of visual experience.

A wide range of picture story books has found favor with older children recently. Noteworthy examples are Allen Say's biography of a Chinese-American bullfighter, *El Chino*; David Macaulay's Caldecott Medal-winning *Black and White*, which tells four different stories simultaneously; and Chris Van Allsburg's *The Mysteries of Harris Burdick*. The latter's vaguely menacing illustrations encourage youngsters of all ages to expand on the brief text passages and invent their own stories.

While the three books just mentioned were all created by illustrators, they can provide stimulation and impetus to writers as well. What qualities make these books work with older children and young adults? First, and most important, none of them is in any way "cute." They aren't about little animals or young children, either; the Chinese bullfighter in *El Chino* starts the book as a boy but soon grows into a man.

The books also embody imaginative concepts that can be appreciated by a broad age range. For example, the scenes in *The Mysteries of Harris Burdick* would no doubt trigger different stories from eight-year-olds than they would from thirteen-year-olds. But both age groups would probably enjoy the book just as much.

10

Visualizing the Picture Book Text

WHETHER YOU'RE PLANNING a pure picture book for younger children or a picture story book for an older audience, your manuscript will have to meet certain basic requirements that are common to all picture books. Here are some hints on how to shape your material so that it will fulfill these requirements.

Think visually

Even if you're not an artist, you should think visually about your story from the start. You may find it useful— many authors have—to type out the texts of several favorite picture books page by page. This should help you to see (a) how economical the writing is; (b) how the stories are paced; and (c) how much the authors left to their illustrators.

You'll probably discover that, especially in stories for younger children, there are few if any passages of straight description. While the author concentrates on the essentials of action and dialogue, it is the illustrator's responsibility to convey the color of a desert sky at night, the other passengers on a crowded bus, or the various flowers in a springtime garden.

Make a dummy of your story

After you've completed the first draft of your story, photocopy the manuscript, mark it as to which passages you think should appear on each page, and then make up a rough dummy of the book. You may never show this dummy to anyone else, but you can learn a lot from it that will help you when you're revising and polishing your manuscript.

Most picture books, as we've said before, are 32 pages long, but the text and illustrations usually occupy no more than 28 of these. The remaining four are taken up with what is known as "front matter." Here, for you to use as a guide when you're making your dummy, is how the sequence generally runs:

Page 1—The half title. The only type on this page is the book's title; sometimes a small spot illustration accompanies it.

Pages 2 and 3—These pages are usually devoted to what is called a "double-spread title page." This simply means that the title type often crosses both pages, with an illustration on page 2, and the author's, illustrator's, and publisher's names on page 3, the right-hand page.

Page 4—The copyright page. The book's copyright notice appears on this page, along with other bibliographical data. If you and the illustrator want to have dedications in the book, they will probably appear on this page also, above the copyright notice.

Pages 5-32—The text and illustrations.

Although the above is the standard page sequence for most picture books, there can be some variations. For instance, room must be left at the end of many nonfiction picture books for the sort of additional material described in Chapter 3, and this often extends the length of the book to 40 or even 48 pages.

Space may have to be reserved for extra items in fictional picture books also. If the book is a retelling of a little-known folk tale from a particular culture, librarians and teachers will expect you to include a note identifying the source. There may be room for this on the copyright page; if not, you and your editor will have to find a spot for it elsewhere.

Or perhaps the story is based on an incident that actually happened to your grandfather or grandmother when they were children. If so, you'll probably want to let readers know this in an Author's Note appearing at either the beginning or end of the book. And a page will have to be set aside for it.

Despite the problems involved with such variations, there are many ways you can make the basic picture book format work in your favor when you're planning and writing the manuscript. For example, knowing that the text begins on page 5 in most picture books, skilled picture book authors will often start their stories with a brief, intriguing paragraph of no more than two or three typewritten lines that they know will fit comfortably on this page. And they make sure that the paragraph contains the sort of action or emotion that will inspire a vivid illustration.

Practiced authors also use the dummy format to help build suspense into their stories. One of the best ways to do this is to take full advantage of the turn from one page to another. For example, in *Three Ducks Went Wandering*, Ron Roy gets his story going in the first few pages when three little ducks disobey their mother and leave the barnyard to see the world. Then Roy uses the page turns to heighten the drama as the little ducks escape from one dangerous situation after another, only to be confronted by an even more dangerous one.

On pages 6 and 7 the ducks have wandered into the enclosure of a big, angry bull. The text reads, "With a snort the bull lowered his head and charged at the ducks," and there's a dramatic illustration by Paul Galdone of the bull coming straight toward the defenseless creatures. Eagerly, the reader turns the page to find out what will happen next and sees a picture of the bull crashing into the fence, while the little ducks waddle safely under the lowest bar.

Child readers and listeners are relieved, of course, but Roy doesn't want them to be *so* relieved that they'll lose interest in the story. So he relies again on the dummy format to generate fresh suspense. On pages 12 and 13, the text reads: "The three ducks gobbled up the grasshoppers, and then went wandering on through the woods, RIGHT IN FRONT OF. . . ." Right in front of what? Once more the reader turns the page to discover what the fearsome creature may be, and interest in the story is securely maintained.

Page turns can help you tell your story in other ways. You can use them to raise the emotional level of a scene: "Ellie raced to the door. . . (Turn the page) . . . and there was Daddy, home at last." They can also make a funny moment even funnier: "Chris and Tony put a seventeenth block on top of their tower. Suddenly it started to topple . . . (Turn the page) . . . and before they could stop it, the whole tower came crashing down." There are all sorts of things you can do with page turns, once you get the knack of working them logically and naturally into your picture book story.

Making a dummy will also help you to pace the story more effectively. If you suddenly find yourself with five paragraphs of text on a page, whereas most of the other pages have had only one or two, chances are the passage would benefit from cutting and tightening. Ask yourself, "Is that paragraph of description really necessary? Does the dialogue between the two boys in the scene go on too long?" Facing the problem in the dummy will enable you to improve the manuscript before you submit it to an editor.

One of the most important pages in any picture book is page 32, the last page. And the most crucial turn of all is the one from page 31 to page 32. Ideally, every picture book should end with a final twist or surprise, and this climactic turn to page 32 is the best place to put it.

A good example can be found in Anna Grossnickle Hines's *It's Just Me, Emily.* All through the book, from morning until mid-afternoon, a mother and her little daughter have been playing an imaginative hide-and-seek guessing game. The daughter makes different animal sounds, the mother guesses what they are, and the little girl says over and over, "No! It's just me, Emily." Then, on pages 30 and 31, the house becomes strangely quiet. The text on page 30 reads, "No thumping or bumping. No howls and no yowls. No giggles or wiggles," and the mother is shown getting up from her sewing machine and looking for Emily.

Under a picture of the mother searching on page 31, the following text appears: "Not a sound . . . not a peep. 'Do you think it could be . . .? Shhhhhh!'" The reader turns to page 32, and Hines delivers the book's final, gentle twist. Both the reader and her mother see Emily napping peacefully on the rug behind a wing chair, and beneath the picture are mother's words: "Yes. It's just Emily."

Depending on the nature of the material, all sorts of twists can make satisfying resolutions for picture book stories. The twist can be as simple as that classic line that ends so many fairy tales: "And they lived happily ever after." Or it can be as complicated as the solution to a picture book mystery. But whatever it is, you should have it in mind from the time you conceive your story. And, whether you make a dummy of your story or not, you should plan for this final twist to appear on page 32—preferably expressed in as few words as possible.

Should I show my dummy to an editor?

Authors often ask if they should submit their rough dummies to editors along with their picture book manuscripts. In most cases, the answer is "No." However, there are some instances when letting the editor know how you visualize the book is absolutely essential.

1. *When the structure and pacing of the story depend on a turn-the-page guessing game format.* For example, when Beatrice Schenk de Regniers submitted the manuscript of *It Does Not Say Meow*, she needed to tell the editor that she intended the clues in verse to appear on a double-page spread, and the name of the animal to be revealed on the spread that followed.

2. *When the identity of an important character or other element is deliberately withheld from the reader,*

but must be known by the illustrator. Eve Bunting had this problem with her story *Scary, Scary Halloween.* She solved it by telling the editor in an introductory note that the characters watching a parade of Halloween trick-or-treaters are a mother cat and her kittens, although readers don't discover this until the book's next-to-last page.

3. *When a significant action is not described in the text, but must be shown in the illustrations.* In Carol Carrick's *Big Old Bones*, the humor springs from the fact that Professor Potts, a pioneer paleontologist, puts together the dinosaur bones he's unearthed in a variety of ways. In the text, he rejects each construction on the ground that no such animal could possibly have existed. But we see from the illustrations that they're actually a triceratops, a brontosaurus, and Tyrannosaurus Rex. Carol Carrick conveyed this necessary information about the professor's mistakes in marginal notes.

Even when explanations like the above are required to make your intentions as an author perfectly clear, try to keep them as short as possible. You don't want to put off editors by making them feel you doubt their ability to visualize the text. Nor do you want to inhibit the imagination of an illustrator by giving him overly detailed instructions.

Picture book authors frequently ask another question: "Should I go a step further and get an artist friend to paint sample illustrations for my story before I submit it to a publisher?" Emphatically, "No." Unless your friend is a professional illustrator and you've worked jointly on the project from its inception, you'll be far better off letting your story speak for itself. Once an editor buys the manuscript, he and his art director will be responsible for finding the best possible illustrator for the book.

The author-illustrator

But what if you are the illustrator as well as the author, as many picture book creators are today? Then, of course, you'll think in terms of a dummy from the very start and sketch in your ideas for illustrations. Some artists do very loose dummy sketches, others make detailed drawings or paintings that could almost serve as finished art. There's no set rule about this; it all depends on how the particular artist prefers to work, and most editors and art directors are comfortable with either approach.

Whether the dummy is loose or detailed, it's also a good idea to do at least two or three sample illustrations to show editors and art directors how you intend the finished book to look. Don't send out the actual samples when you submit the manuscript, however; there's too much danger that they'll be damaged in handling or become dogeared. Enclose good color photographs or photocopies of the samples instead, and submit them with a clear photocopy of the dummy—not the original. In the cover letter, tell the editor what you're doing and explain that the photocopies don't mean it's a simultaneous submission. At the same time, you can offer to send the editor the originals if he's seriously interested in the project.

11

The Pros and Cons of Writing Picture Books in Verse

M ANY NOVICE picture book authors are troubled by a hard-to-decide question when they sit down at their typewriters or word processors: Should I write my story in prose or verse? Rightly or wrongly, a sizable number choose the latter course. Of the thousands of picture book submissions that publishers receive in any given year, probably a quarter to a third are written in verse.

Some are collections of original poems that the authors hope to see published in anthology form with colorful illustrations. Unfortunately, the market for such picture book anthologies is extremely limited unless (a) the author already has an established reputation as a children's poet, or (b) the poems center on a popular theme, like holidays or the seasons, and are of truly exceptional quality.

Many authors decide to write their picture book manuscripts, both fantasies and realistic stories, in verse form. The decision probably stems from the authors' observation of their target audience. For almost from babyhood, and certainly from the time they first hear "Mother Goose," children everywhere respond to the rhythms, repeated patterns, and rhyme schemes of poetry.

Theodor Geisel (Dr. Seuss) was well aware of this when he wrote *The Cat in the Hat* and his other tremendously popular stories in lilting couplets that use the simplest words. After observing a child's delighted reaction to one of Seuss's books, it's easy to understand why an aspiring writer for children might decide to try his hand at something similar. It looks so easy. What these people fail to realize is that writing good poetry in any form is extremely difficult, and writing a complete story in verse is probably the most difficult task of all.

It can be done. Eve Bunting, in her picture book *Scary, Scary Halloween*, sets the tone and style of the entire story with this opening stanza:

> I peer outside, there's something there
> That makes me shiver, spikes my hair.
> It must be Halloween.

Note how the author uses very simple language, then injects an unusual verb in the phrase "spikes my hair." That sort of verbal play is not only permitted but desirable in poetry.

Note, too, how the stanza, in just seventeen words, sets up a dramatic situation, generates suspense, and creates a vivid scene for an artist to illustrate. That's what the beginning of every picture book text, whether written in poetry or prose, should ideally achieve. But few accomplish it as swiftly and sparingly as does *Scary, Scary Halloween*. That's probably because Eve Bunting understands that the verse form, when handled deftly, requires an author to write in a more compressed and economical style.

Verse also allows an author to reach for dramatic effects in language that might seem overdone if written in prose. Here's an example from a later passage in *Scary, Scary Halloween*.

> Thunder, thunder up above!
> "What is it, Mother?" "Shh, my love!
> It's just the thump of creature feet,
> A creature in a winding sheet,
> His claws are dragging on the floor.
> He's crashing, smashing at the door!"
> "Will he find us here, below?"
> "Shh, my love, I cannot know."

To justify such heightened language, an author needs a powerful dramatic situation at the core of the story. *Scary, Scary Halloween* has such a situation: It's a fantasy about four pairs of green eyes that watch a parade of fearsome creatures go past the house where they're hiding under the porch. Only at the end, as we said earlier, does the author confirm what bright youngsters will have guessed all along: that the creatures are Halloween trick-or-treaters, and the green eyes belong to a mother cat and her three kittens.

But a larger-than-life situation is not always necessary. The casual lyrics of a Dorothy Parker or an Ogden

Nash make their points neatly and wittily even as they tell a story. And the same effect can be achieved in a picture book text for children. Beatrice Schenk de Regniers has done it in many books, including *So Many Cats*. Just look at (and real aloud) these lines from the latter story:

> We had a cat—
> an Only Cat.
> She was a sad
> and lonely cat.
> So when a very hungry cat
> came making a great din,
> meowing, mewing
> scratching at our door,
> we thought
> this could be the very cat
> to make our cat a happy cat,
> and so we let her in—
> little knowing we were getting more
> than we had
> bargained
> for.

The tone here is so natural and conversational that you may not even be conscious that the author is writing in verse until you suddenly become aware of the clever internal rhyme scheme. The text also does much more than simply display her skill as a poet. It immediately characterizes the unnamed child narrator as a warm, perceptive cat-lover with a dry sense of humor. And, like *Scary, Scary Halloween* and all good picture book texts, it offers one opportunity after another for lively, active illustrations.

It's instructive for an aspiring writer of stories in

verse to read about successful books like these two. But
what other practical steps can you take to help you save
time and avoid making mistakes when you sit down to
write your own stories? Here are a few suggestions:

1. To find out what verse stories are being published
for children today, go to the children's department of
your local library or to a good children's bookstore and
ask for a list of recommended titles. Analyze the books,
as we've done with *Scary, Scary Halloween* and *So
Many Cats*, to see how the authors achieve their effects.
No doubt you'll discover some approaches and techniques that you can apply to your own writing.

2. After examining a wide variety of books, you may
decide your poetic skills are rusty and need sharpening.
Perhaps you wrote a lot of poetry in high school and
college, but that was a long time ago. If so, it may be
worthwhile for you to take a course in poetry writing at
your local college, university, or adult education center.
What you learn about different verse forms and how to
write them will extend your poetic range and enable you
to tell your story in more than just rhyming couplets.

3. Use whatever poetic form you select to help you
tell your story more dramatically or humorously. In an
effort to maintain a rhyming scheme, don't get so involved in the form itself that every other element—characterization, plot, etc.—is sacrificed to it. Too many
verse stories by beginning authors run on to ten or
twelve pages because the author has become more concerned with maintaining a poetic pattern than with telling the story.

It's important to remember that a story in verse
should observe the same rules as any other picture book

text. If it's aimed at quite young children, like *Scary, Scary Halloween*, it should be no more than two or three double-spaced typewritten manuscript pages. If it's intended for a slightly older audience of, say, five-to-eight-year-olds, like *So Many Cats*, it can be as long as five or six manuscript pages.

Whatever the length, it should—like other picture books—have characters that the reader can care about, a strong plot with a beginning, middle, and end, and if possible, a final surprise twist at the end. No restless youngster is going to sit still for rhythm and rhyme if there's nothing else in the story to hold his attention.

Maybe, after deciding to write your story in verse and doing several drafts of it, you become discouraged. The rhymes seem forced, and you feel as if you're losing your grip on the story line. What should you do? Stop work on the story and put it in a drawer until inspiration strikes again? Or try a different approach?

The latter course would probably be the best. For, as many successful authors have discovered, stories for children can be rhythmic without being written in verse. The trick is to write them in lyrical prose—and the result is often more effective.

What exactly is lyrical prose? It's prose that incorporates many of the characteristics of poetry for children, including rhythm, repetition, and the use of unusual, vivid words to add flavor to the text. Most important of all, it's *speakable*. In an era when more and more parents are reading aloud to their children from the time they're babies, the speakability of a picture book story has become even more essential than it was in the past.

Let's look at some good examples of lyrical, speakable

prose. Here's one from the opening of *The Half-Birthday Party* by Charlotte Pomerantz:

> One day, when Daniel's sister Katie
> was six months old,
> She stood for the first time.
> She took hold of a table leg
> and pulled herself up.
> "Daddy, Mommy, come quick," said Daniel.
> "Katie is standing."
>
> That evening, Daniel decided
> to give Katie a half-birthday party.
> He sent an invitation to Lily,
> his friend across the hall.
> And one to Grandma and Mr. Bangs,
> who always came to parties with her.
> The invitation read:
>
> My sister Katie is six months old.
> Please come to her half-birthday party
> on Sunday afternoon at 3 o'clock.
> And bring half a present.
>
> Daniel
>
> P.S. You have to tell a whole story
> about the half present.

In this relatively brief passage, the author accomplishes a great deal. She gets the story moving right away by establishing Daniel's pride in his little sister when she stands for the first time, and his idea for the half-birthday party. And she does it in simple but rhythmic prose. Try reading the passage aloud and you'll see just how speakable it is.

Lyrical prose can be used to achieve many different kinds of effects. Carol Carrick employs it in her picture story book, *Dark and Full of Secrets*, to create a mood of foreboding and suspense. Here's how the story begins:

> Early morning mist rose from the pond like steam from a witch's brew. Christopher's father held the canoe steady. Just as Christopher was climbing in, his dog Ben jumped in with him, making the boat rock.
>
> "Ben!" Christopher yelled, pushing the dog out.
>
> "Home, Ben! Go home!" his father ordered, pointing toward the house. Ben slunk away.
>
> "Today will be a scorcher," Christopher's father said as they pushed off. "A good day for swimming."
>
> "I don't like to go in the pond," said Christopher. "There are things in there, and the bottom is all mucky."
>
> It wasn't that Christopher didn't like swimming. In the ocean the waves rose green like glass and, when they broke over him, the sudsy foam made him tingle. But the pond was dark and full of secrets.

Note how the author, although writing in prose, weaves in poetic imagery to add color to her language. Instead of simply stating "Early morning mist rose from the pond" and leaving it at that, she goes on to say that it rose "like steam from a witch's brew." And see how she builds a rhythmic flow in the last paragraph of the passage, culminating in the description of the pond as being "dark and full of secrets." This may be prose, but it hooks a reader with all the force and imagination of poetry.

Whether you're writing lyrical prose or actual poetry, how can you test your own writing to make sure it's as imaginative—and "speakable"—as possible? Here are some ideas that have worked well for other authors, and should work for you, too.

1. Go over the completed draft of your manuscript and look critically at all the images you've used. Are they fresh or flat? If you decide that too many of them fall in the second category, try to think of better ones. Don't strain for an effect, but at the same time don't miss a chance to leave an impression on the reader, either.

2. Reread your story and ask yourself the following questions: Does the writing flow smoothly from one sentence and paragraph to another, with breaks in the rhythm here and there when something exciting or funny happens? Or does it contain too many stiff and awkward stretches?

If you're unsure about the latter, try reading the story aloud, either to yourself or to a sympathetic listener. If you still have difficulty judging whether the text speaks well or not, record it and play back the tape. As you listen, mark those places in the manuscript that seem jerky, or that don't make their points as clearly and sharply as you would like. Those are the sections that you should revise and polish before you send the manuscript to a publisher.

12

From Submission to Contract

A T LAST, AFTER LONG HOURS of hard work at your desk, you've completed your picture book, nonfiction proposal, or novel. You're naturally excited, but at the same time you wonder if, in the rush to finish it, you've lost perspective on the material. So you put it aside for a few days or a week and then reread it slowly and thoughtfully. After making a few final changes, you feel your manuscript is ready to send out into the world, or at least as ready as you can make it. What's the best way to go about this?

Before submitting their manuscripts to publishers, some authors wonder if they should protect their ownership of the material by copyrighting the manuscripts as unpublished works with the Register of Copyrights at the Library of Congress in Washington, D.C. In my opinion, this is an unnecessary step and expense. Under the 1978 Copyright Act, all "original works of authorship" have automatic copyright protection from the moment they are "fixed in any tangible medium of expression." This protection lasts for the author's lifetime, plus fifty years. After a book is published, it becomes the publisher's responsibility to copyright it as a published work. In the case of most children's books, the copyright for the text is taken out in the author's name.

Now back to the submission process. Ideally you should have done the necessary homework beforehand so that as soon as the manuscript is finished you can send it off to the first publishing house on your list. But whether you do it in advance or after the manuscript is typed, here are the steps you should take in order to handle the submission process as efficiently—and effectively—as possible.

The submission process

1. It probably goes without saying, but the first thing you should do is prepare a clean, double-spaced copy of the manuscript. If you type it, make several photocopies and submit one of them; it'll save you retyping time later if you hold on to the original. Just be sure to let the editor know that, although the manuscript has been photocopied, it's an exclusive submission.

If you work on a word processor, use a letter-quality printer for your manuscript. Editors react negatively to the pale, dot matrix type produced by inferior machines and often put off reading such manuscripts.

2. Study publishers' current catalogues in the children's department of your local library (most librarians keep copies), or write directly to the publishers for them. Look, too, at the publishers' seasonal list ads that appear in trade magazines, such as *School Library Jour-*

nal and *Publishers Weekly.* Those in the latter publication can be found in the special children's book issues that come out in February to announce spring titles and in July to herald the new fall books.

When you have a feel for the different publishing houses and what types of books they do, you'll have a much better idea of which houses might be interested in your manuscript. You should then read some books published by these houses in order to confirm that your instincts were right.

3. Once you've decided on the publishers you want to submit your manuscript to, in order of preference, you'll need to find the names of the children's book editors. These can be located in *Literary Market Place* (published annually by R. R. Bowker Publishing and available in the reference departments of most libraries) or the market listings published regularly in *The Writer* Magazine, *The Writer's Handbook* (updated annually), and by such organizations as the Society of Children's Book Writers and Illustrators.

A word about the Society (22736 Vanowen Street, Suite 106, West Hills, California 91307). With over 5,000 members, it is the largest organization in the country devoted solely to the needs and interests of children's book authors and illustrators. An author can join the Society as an associate member before he has had anything published and receive its bimonthly *Bulletin*, which contains the latest market listings, as well as listings of children's book publishers, editors, and art directors that are updated annually. These lists can be invaluable in light of the high degree of editorial turnover that has occurred in the children's book field in recent years, making many other lists obsolete almost before they're printed.

4. When you study market listings, you will find the following statement after the names of some publishers: "Not accepting unsolicited submissions at the present time." This means that the publishers in question will read only those manuscripts submitted by literary agents, and if you send them your manuscript directly it will be returned unopened and unread.

As this policy has spread, more and more children's book authors are asking: *"Is it necessary to have an agent in order to get published?"* My answer is no, for several reasons. To begin with, the number of experienced, knowledgeable agents who handle children's books exclusively is still small, and few of them have room on their client lists for newcomers unless they come highly recommended. Numerous other agents handle some children's book writers, but the bulk of their time and effort is devoted to their writers for adults.

If you remain unconvinced and are determined to acquire an agent, you can find many listed in *Literary Market Place;* in a circular published by the Association of Authors' Representatives (10 Astor Pl., 3rd Floor, New York, NY 10003); and in other reference sources, with notations as to whether or not they are open to children's material and how they want to be approached—in most cases via a query letter. However, since the majority of children's book publishers are still reading and considering unsolicited manuscripts, I generally advise beginning authors to concentrate their energies on finding a publisher rather than an agent. If a manuscript has promise, chances are that editors will respond favorably to it, and acceptance is likely to come more quickly than if the author had spent months trying to find an agent first.

5. While most publishers continue to read unsolicited

manuscripts, some qualify this policy by stating that they want to receive the complete manuscripts only of picture books. On all nonfiction projects and on longer fiction manuscripts of, say, fifty or more pages, they prefer to get query letters first. Other publishers may say that they want to see outlines and two or three sample chapters of novels. (Virtually no one asks for a query letter or outline on a picture book unless it's part of a board book series; the query letter might be longer than the actual text!)

These are simply time-saving devices, and they're usually helpful to everyone concerned. With publishers receiving more and more submissions each year, it's much easier and quicker for them to decide from a query letter or sample chapters whether a novel would be right for the list than to log in and read a 200-page manuscript.

Nonfiction query letters and what they should include were discussed in Chapter 2. *But how do you write an effective query letter for a novel?* Here are a few tips:

(a) In the opening paragraph, tell what category the story falls into—mystery, adventure, humorous, animal, etc.—give the title, and say what age group it's aimed at.

(b) Go on to provide some idea of the story's content. This needn't be a complete, detailed synopsis of the plot; in fact, it probably shouldn't be. But it should convey who the main character is, what he or she is striving for, some of the obstacles—scary or funny—that have to be overcome along the way, and whether or not the character succeeds in the end.

(c) Include a rundown of your publishing credits, highlighting those that are especially relevant to your new manuscript; for example, previous novels (and publishers) or short stories in a similar vein that have appeared in children's magazines.

If you don't have any credits yet, say that, too. The editor won't hold it against you, since he knows that everyone has to start somewhere.

(d) End the letter with a simple question: "Would you be interested in seeing the outline and sample chapters of my novel, or the complete manuscript?"

If possible, try to confine your query letter to one, or at most two, single-spaced typewritten pages. And be sure to include a self-addressed, stamped envelope when you mail it off to an editor.

6. Make copies of your query letters and use them to start a submission file on your book. Some authors also like to maintain a file card record on each of their manuscripts, with entries of when and to whom it was sent out and when it came back, but I personally find that a file folder is enough. Besides copies of your own letters, you should also keep every editorial response you get to the manuscript. In this way, you'll have a complete submission history of the project in case you need to refer to it at some later date.

One final word about query letters: Most children's book editors don't mind receiving a simultaneous query letter, that is, one being sent to several other editors at the same time.

7. When an editor responds favorably to your query, it's time to get the manuscript ready to mail. If you receive more than one positive response, send the manuscript to the publisher you prefer and hold the other letters for future follow-up in case the first publisher declines it.

8. *Should you write a cover letter to accompany the manuscript?* Some say it's better to let the material

speak for itself, but I happen to like cover letters, and so do many other editors. They're essential when a manuscript is being submitted at the editor's invitation, for they'll remind him of your original query, which he probably has in a "pending" file. They also serve a useful purpose if they accompany a direct submission like a picture book story . . . as long as they're brief and to the point.

Since the editor-author relationship is a highly personal one, you can make use of the cover letter to introduce yourself to the editor as a literate, caring human being. Besides giving the title and category of your manuscript in the first sentence, you can go on to say in a few carefully chosen words what impelled you to write it, and then you can list your relevant writing credits if you have some.

9. Whether or not you include a cover letter, you should *pack your manuscript carefully before sending it off.* As an editor I'm constantly surprised by the authors who simply fold up their picture book manuscripts and stick them into #10 envelopes or put heavy rubber bands around the pages of their novels and then shove them into jiffy bags. Such treatment virtually guarantees that the manuscript will arrive at the publisher's office in a torn or disheveled condition. Why not put your manuscript into a file folder or, in the case of a novel, two folders before mailing it? That won't add much to the weight of the package, and your submission will make a much better impression when it's opened in the editor's office.

If you want the editor to acknowledge receipt of the manuscript, enclose a stamped, self-addressed postcard with a line for the editorial department to fill in, saying they received the manuscript on such-and-such a date.

In any case, be sure to enclose a stamped, self-addressed envelope or jiffy bag (same size as you used for submission) for the return of the manuscript if it doesn't meet the editor's needs.

10. *What about multiple submissions—sending the manuscript to more than one editor at the same time?* Some authors urge this as a means of speeding up the reading process and getting a quicker decision. Like many other editors, I resent the practice because I've been burned by multiple submissions on more than one occasion. I've paid for outside readings on a manuscript and have written encouragingly to an author, only to have the author tell me that he has already sold his material elsewhere.

Now, if I know or suspect that a manuscript is a multiple submission, I read a few pages of it, and if it doesn't seem right for our list, send it back immediately without giving it a full reading. Why invest a lot of time and effort in a submission that isn't exclusively ours?

11. A much more effective way to get a prompt reaction from an editor, in my opinion, is to *follow up diligently on your submissions.* What's a reasonable waiting time for a decision? Because of the small editorial staffs in most children's book departments, it's usually four to eight weeks for a picture book manuscript or nonfiction proposal, six weeks to three months for a longer fiction manuscript. Whether the wait is shorter or longer generally depends on how many readings the manuscript is given.

If you haven't heard from the publisher in a reasonable length of time, write a letter of inquiry, enclosing another stamped, self-addressed postcard. Wait several more weeks, and if the publisher hasn't replied, telephone the editorial department and ask about the status of your manuscript. Then, if you still don't receive a satisfactory response to your inquiries, write the editor a polite note saying that since you haven't heard from him, you've decided to withdraw your manuscript from consideration in order to submit it elsewhere. Send this by certified mail, with a return receipt requested.

Editors' letters and how to interpret them

Many authors are confused by editors' rejection letters, and don't know how to interpret them. Sometimes letters of encouragement can be puzzling, too; authors aren't sure how seriously they should take them. Here is a brief guide to the various types of letters an editor writes when he returns a manuscript, and what each of them usually means.

1. The printed form rejection slip. This is just what it seems—a flat rejection. The editor simply couldn't use your manuscript, and with four thousand or more submissions crowding into his office each year, neither he nor anyone on his staff had the time to write you a personal letter.

2. Sometimes, though, you'll find a handwritten note scrawled at the bottom of the rejection slip—"Nice touches of humor (or suspense or drama). Try us again." This probably means that the editor or his first reader liked some things about your manuscript and is inviting you to make other submissions. If you get such a note, take the person who wrote it at his word and send him another manuscript.

3. Perhaps you'll get a similarly encouraging personal letter, signed by the editor, in which he comments briefly on your manuscript, wishes you luck in placing it elsewhere, and invites you to submit more material. This

means that the editor himself read your manuscript and saw something in it. While a letter like this is far from an acceptance, it shouldn't be dismissed either, for no busy editor takes the time to write such a note unless he sees promise in an author's work.

4. Then there's the much longer letter that you may get in which the editor goes into detail about what he likes and doesn't like in the manuscript, makes specific suggestions for improving it, and says that he'll be happy to read the manuscript again if you decide to revise it. Such a letter means exactly what it says—that the editor is serious about your manuscript and thinks it may find a place on his list if you correct its weaknesses through revision.

How should you respond to such a letter? To begin with, you shouldn't ignore it or set it aside, even though the idea of getting back into the manuscript and making extensive changes may seem daunting. Next, you should evaluate the editor's suggestions carefully, decide if you agree with them, and then write the editor a letter. Thank him for taking an interest in your manuscript, and then go on to tell him your reactions to his suggestions. Perhaps you disagree with some of them; if so, be direct about it and explain your reasons. On the other hand, his comments may have sparked ideas for different ways to solve the problems in the manuscript. Share these with him; it will help to get an author-editor discussion going.

If you've decided you want to revise the manuscript, let the editor know how long you think the revision will take you to do. Don't feel you have to get the manuscript back to him within a week. If he's genuinely interested in your material—and you have to assume he is—he won't forget it so quickly. And he'll have more respect for you as an author if he senses you'll spend the time needed to think through the revisions instead of making them hastily and rushing the manuscript back to him. Some authors have told me that they're reluctant to make major revisions on speculation without any assurance that they'll eventually get a contract for the manuscript. Of course that has to be an individual decision, and it can be especially difficult for an established author who's used to receiving a contract before revisions. But for a beginning author, I believe it's generally worth the gamble, and I can speak from personal experience in this regard. For my first book, *The Scarecrow Book*, my collaborator Dale Ferguson and I did three sets of sample material before the editor was convinced the project deserved a contract. Looking back now, I'm glad we did, for the process helped us sharpen the focus of the book.

I asked Mary Downing Hahn for four revisions of her first novel, *The Sara Summer*, before we decided the story would make a successful book. The author said she learned a lot about both writing and editing from this experience and I certainly gained a greater respect for her as an author. Moreover, it led to an ongoing editor-author relationship, as she and I worked together on many more novels—none of which required as many revisions as *The Sara Summer*.

Finally, after who knows how many submissions and perhaps as many revisions, there comes that exciting day when you open a new letter from the editor and read: "We're happy to tell you that your manuscript seems in solid shape now and we would like to contract it for publication."

After reveling in unabashed euphoria for a while, and calling your husband, wife, mother, or best friend to tell them the exciting news, you sit down to read the contract terms outlined in the rest of the letter. You may find some of these terms hard to understand—many first-time authors do. But the key provisions in a standard book contract really aren't that difficult to grasp, as we'll see in the next chapter.

13

From Contract to Publication—and Beyond

S OME PUBLISHERS' CONTRACTS are long, others are
shorter, but in either case most of the pages are
filled with what are known in the trade as "boilerplate
clauses." These concern such things as the author's responsibility to protect the publisher from a libel suit,
what will happen if the author fails to deliver the manuscript or the publisher fails to publish it, and how the
author can regain his rights in the work if the book goes
out of print.

If you have an agent, he will negotiate the contract
with the publisher and explain any confusing terms or
clauses to you. An author who doesn't have an agent
may think he should have a lawyer look over the contract
for him. Since few lawyers are experienced in literary

and copyright law, they are not likely to be too helpful. In most instances, you'll probably be better off if you read the contract carefully yourself, make a list of those points that aren't clear, and discuss them with your editor or someone in the publisher's contract department. In the meantime, here are the key points you should look for first in any contract:

1. *How you will be paid for your material.* Most children's book publishers offer an *advance against royalties,* but some may offer you a *flat fee.* In the latter arrangement, you'll be paid a certain amount for all rights to your material, and will receive no further income from it, no matter how many copies the book sells. Established authors usually refuse to accept flat-fee contracts, but if you're just starting out and have tried to place the manuscript at a number of houses, you may feel that it's more important to get it published than to hold out for a royalty contract. In any case, there's no harm in asking the publisher if there's a possibility of getting a royalty on the book when sales reach a certain point . . . say, 3% of the list price after 10,000 copies have been sold. The worst he can say is "No."

If you're offered an advance against royalties, the size of the advance will depend on what type of book your project is.

In recent years, the typical hardcover advance on a picture book text by a new author was in the neighborhood of $2000–$2500, while the advance on a first novel ranged from $2500–$4000. Advances have gradually risen along with hardcover book prices and the economy in general, so it's safe to assume that they'll continue to rise in the future.

Royalties also depend on the nature of the book. The customary royalty for a new author is 10% of the book's catalogue list price, but in the case of a picture book the author shares this royalty with the illustrator, each of them receiving 5%. On nonfiction photo essays, the royalty is usually divided 50/50 between the author and photographer. And if a novel or nonfiction project requires some illustrations, the author may be asked to take a royalty of 7% or 8% so that the illustrator can be given a 2% or 3% royalty. As a consequence, only the author of an unillustrated novel can be pretty sure of getting the full 10% royalty.

Some publishers base the author's royalty on the net amount the book brings in after discount rather than the list price. A bit of arithmetic will show that a net royalty contract is much less advantageous to the author. Say the book carries a retail or list price of $14.00, and your royalty is 10% of list; that means you'll be earning $1.40 on each copy sold. However, if you have a net royalty, and the average discount on the book to retailers and wholesalers is 40% or 50%, you'll receive only 84¢ or 70¢ per copy sold.

You may grumble about this, but you're not likely to budge a net royalty publisher from his position, especially if you're a new author with no sales track record. As with flat fee contracts, you'll have to base your decision on whether or not to accept a net royalty on how enthusiastic you feel about the particular publisher, and whether you think it's the best home you can find for your manuscript.

Established author friends may tell you that they're receiving a sliding scale royalty on their books and urge you to ask your publisher for the same. You can ask, but you'll almost certainly be turned down, for no author is given a sliding scale until he's proven his mettle by delivering a string of successful books. What exactly is a sliding scale royalty? Basically it's an increase in the royalty rate from 10% to 12½% of the list price on novels or, in the case of picture books and photo essays, from 5% to 6¼%, with the rise occurring after a certain number of copies of the book have been sold. This breaking point may be as low as 7500 copies in the case of a novel or as high as 15,000 copies on a full-color picture book, where the publisher's initial production costs are much steeper.

Whether you have a standard royalty or a sliding scale contract, the book will have to sell enough copies to earn back the initial advance before you get any additional royalties.

Using a $14.00 list price again, and assuming that the book is a novel for which you received an advance of $3000 against a royalty of 10%, your break-even point on the book would be sales of approximately 2150 copies. In the case of a first book, that point probably won't be reached until six months or more after the book's publication. On all sales after that, you'll receive your $1.40 royalty per book.

Most publishers compute and pay royalties twice a year on sales in the preceding six months, which is why I often say to authors that books are like bonds, and royalty checks like interest payments. Only a few children's book authors and illustrators get rich from their work, but those who produce a steady stream of successful titles can, in time, make a comfortable income.

2. The next clauses you should look for in a royalty contract are those that tell you *what percentage you will receive of the income from subsidiary rights*. These rights include the possible sale of your book to a book club, a paperback reprinter, a foreign publisher, a textbook anthology, a filmstrip or audio-tape producer, and

in the case of a few junior novels, a television or movie producer. There are also electronic rights, which promise to play an increasingly important role in the juvenile rights picture.

Although subsidiary rights deals in the children's book field rarely command the spectacular advances that make news in adult publishing, some children's book authors—especially of fiction—earn hefty amounts of money from the sale of subsidiary rights in their books.

If you have an agent, he will handle the foreign and audio-visual rights in your book, while the publisher takes care of domestic book clubs and paperback reprinters. If you don't have an agent, the publisher will be responsible for selling all of the subsidiary rights in the property, often with the aid of agents abroad. Trust him to do the best job he can with the book; not only does he have the necessary expertise, but he also stands to make a profit on each sale.

The division of subsidiary rights income between author and publisher varies somewhat from house to house, but here are some standard splits against which you can compare those in your contract:

(a) *Book clubs, paperback reprints, and sales to textbook publishers:* 50% to the author, 50% to the publisher (or, in the case of a picture book, 25% to the author and 25% to the illustrator).

(b) *Foreign sales:* 75% to the author and 25% to the publisher (or, with a picture book, 37½% to the author and 37½% to the illustrator).

(c) *Film rights:* 80% or 90% to the author; 10% or 20% to the publisher. (Since film rights are usually sold only on novels, which are not illustrated, the author generally receives the entire share.)

Once you've established a firm reputation with a publisher, you may be able to negotiate some of these percentages upward, especially those covering foreign and film rights. But, along with the advance and the royalty rate on the publisher's edition, the subsidiary rights percentages in most first book contracts are not negotiable.

3. *The option clause.* This clause gives the publisher the right of first refusal on your next children's book manuscript, and sometimes on your next two manuscripts. Most editors insist that first-time authors agree to the inclusion of an option clause in the contract, and actually, I feel it's to the author's advantage, since it confirms the publisher's ongoing interest in the author's work. However, once an author becomes established and perhaps begins to publish with more than one house, he generally asks that the option be struck out of his contracts.

The clause isn't all that restrictive in any case. If an author is terribly unhappy with an editor or publisher, he can always pull an old manuscript out of the drawer, submit it as his next project, and rejoice in being a free agent again when the manuscript is rejected.

4. *The clause regarding permissions.* If you quote from published material in your manuscript, you should pay special attention to the clause—standard in most contracts—that states you are responsible for obtaining permission to reprint these extracts in your book and paying any fees that may be involved. Written permission is usually required only for passages of more than fifty words from books or magazines published within the past fifty years or so, but if you're in any doubt as to whether you need to get clearance, it's best to write to the permissions departments of the publishers in question.

In my experience, the steepest fees are often charged for the use of lines from contemporary song lyrics and poems by well-known present-day authors. If these, and other, permissions fees seem onerous to you, you may decide to paraphrase the quotations involved or even omit them from your manuscript.

On to publication

Once the contract has been negotiated and signed, and you've received your advance, what happens next? And what role will you be expected to play in the development of the book?

At some point you're sure to receive a request from the editorial or publicity department for biographical information and a photograph. Take your time with this, and answer the publisher's questions as fully as possible. He'll especially welcome anecdotes about your background and where you got the idea for the book that can be woven into the jacket copy. Provide him also with a photograph that does you justice; as an editor, I know how disappointing it is when a new author sends in an out-of-focus snapshot that could never be used on the jacket or in any other publicity material.

On some biographical questionnaires there's space for the author to write a brief description of his book. Try to make this summary as lively and intriguing as you can, for the editor may well use it—or parts of it—on the front jacket flap of the book or in the announcement catalogue.

On a novel or nonfiction book, the editor will send you the copyeditor's queries to go over and answer. These generally concern minor matters of styling and punctuation consistency, but sometimes the copyeditor will ask you to clarify a point or rewrite a confusing passage. As with any revision suggestions, you should examine the pages in question, try to see what the copyeditor is getting at, and go along with all of his suggestions that seem reasonable. For his aim, like yours, is to make the book as good as it can be.

If you've written a picture book, the editor may, as a courtesy, show you samples of the illustrator's work or even a copy of the dummy to check for accuracy of detail. But you won't have approval of the illustrator, nor will you or any author have approval of the jacket design for your book. Those creative decisions are made by the editor and the art director, and at some houses, members of the marketing department staff have a say in them also.

After the manuscript has been copyedited and designed, the next stage in any book is galley or page proofs. These are uncorrected proofs of the text. For a picture book, there may be only one sheet; for a teenage novel as many as 150. In any case, you'll receive a set to read, correct, and return to the publisher. A professional proofreader and probably the editor will be reading them, too, and the aim of all these readings is to catch as many typographical errors as possible.

Some authors, when they go over the proofs, suddenly decide they'd like to rewrite entire passages of their books. It's wise to restrain such impulses and limit yourself to a few spots that, for one reason or another, you feel should be polished or clarified. If you don't restrain yourself your editor will, for it costs a great deal to reset large chunks of type (and some contracts call for all or part of these costs to be charged to the author).

Following the proofs come repros and other production stages that you probably won't be involved in. Then the book will be presented to the house's sales representatives at the seasonal sales conference. Most children's book departments participate in two of these conferences each year, one in April or May at which the new titles to be published in the fall are described enthusiastically by the editor, and another in December at which all the spring titles are introduced.

Jacket proofs of the new books are prepared for these conferences so the sales reps will have something to show their customers, and proofs of the interiors of picture books and some heavily illustrated nonfiction books are handed out also. After the conference, your editor will probably send you the jacket proof for your book, or complete proofs—called "folded and gathered sheets"—of your picture book, and then it'll be time for oo-ing and ah-ing. (But if you or the editor catch a typo on the jacket, or in the picture book, you'll still be able to correct it.)

Finally, several months after the sales conference in most instances, the great day arrives when you receive the first bound copy of your book in the mail. It will be followed shortly by your other free author's copies, generally ten or fifteen in all, depending on the number specified in your contract. Picture book authors may get fewer free copies because, like the royalty, these are usually divided with the illustrator. But all authors and illustrators receive a discount on additional copies of the book that they wish to purchase.

Now comes the exciting—and scary—time of waiting for reviews of the book. The most influential are not, as you might suppose, the ones that run in major national consumer publications, such as *The New York Times Book Review*. Instead, they're those that appear in four literary and review periodicals, unknown to most laymen, but held in high esteem by public and school librarians. The four periodicals are:

School Library Journal
The Booklist of the American Library Association
The Bulletin of the Center for Children's Books, published by the University of Illinois at Urbana
Horn Book

As they pursue their careers in children's books, many authors subscribe to one or more of these periodicals as a way to keep up with what's going on in the field. *Horn Book* is the most "literary" of the publications, with articles in each issue by authors, illustrators, and critics, as well as reviews of recommended current books, while *School Library Journal*, which prints unfavorable reviews along with favorable notices, offers the most comprehensive review coverage.

When their books are published, many new authors feel they should do something on their own to help promote them. Some dream of being interviewed on national television, others have the more realistic expectation of an autograph signing at a local bookstore. Such publicity efforts boost an author's ego, but they don't usually generate many sales—especially of a first book. Far more crucial to the success of any children's book are favorable reviews in the four periodicals mentioned above, followed up by other recommendations and purchases by school and public libraries across the country. The latter are generated by the 400-plus review copies of each new juvenile title that the publisher sends out to major library systems, such as the Los Angeles County Board of Education; the Public Library of Atlanta, Georgia; and the State Department of Education in Augusta, Maine.

These promotional mailings are bolstered, of course, by the efforts of the publisher's sales reps to get a good selection of each season's books into bookstores everywhere. But authors, illustrators, and editors have to accept a basic reality of the business: Most bookstores, even the specialty children's bookshops that have sprung up in recent years, devote the bulk of their shelf space to colorfully illustrated picture and gift books and paperback reprints, and have room for only a relatively small number of hardcover fiction and nonfiction titles. So don't be surprised, or unduly disappointed, if you don't find your book in any local stores.

Both new and well-known authors often ask me how long they can expect to see their books remain in print. That's an almost impossible question to answer in a general way. A few books quickly establish themselves as outstanding examples of their kind and stay in print for decades. But most books have a much shorter life span. If they receive good reviews in the library media, they'll probably enjoy solid sales for several years, and then experience a dropoff, more drastic in some cases than others. Then it's up to the individual publisher to decide whether he can afford to keep the book going with a small reprint, or whether, however reluctantly, he'll have to let it go out of print. It's probably safe to say that most hardcover children's books stay in print for at least two to three years, and many titles rack up life spans of six to eight years or more.

In the meantime, one hopes the authors have gone on to write and publish other books. For many authors, the second book is the hardest. They're afraid they won't be able to recapture whatever it was that made the first book a success. The one bit of advice I give authors in this dilemma is to relax, forget there was a previous book, and treat the second book as if it were the first. For the truth is that every new book you write *is* in some way a first book, no matter how many titles you may have to your credit.

As your career develops, there are several pitfalls you should do your best to avoid. If you are still trying to place your first book, you may find it hard to believe, but there could come a time—if you are prolific—when you'll find yourself signing contracts with three or more different publishers. There's nothing intrinsically wrong with this; however, you may one day feel that you've spread yourself too thin.

On the other hand, in the existing publishing climate, you shouldn't rely too heavily on any one house or editor, either. Back in the 1950s and 1960s, independent publishers abounded and once a children's book editor became the head of a department, he tended to stay in the job until he retired. That's no longer the case. Currently, mergers and acquisitions are commonplace in publishing, and children's book editors seem to be in constant motion.

This editorial flux has had a devastating effect on authors, both beginning and well-established. Sometimes a new author has rejoiced when an editor has bought his first book, only to learn a few months later that that editor has left, and his replacement has no interest in the book and wants to cancel the contract. Or an established author who's published a string of successful novels with a particular editor is shocked when his successor declines the author's latest effort with a terse letter that's little more than a form rejection.

As authors attempt to steer their way through the

treacherous undercurrents of today's publishing scene, they may fall victim to depression and despair. It's easy to lose your confidence when acceptance suddenly turns to rejection. If that occurs, the only thing to do is try to maintain your sense of perspective while you assess where you are as a writer, and plot a new course of action.

Sometimes this may mean, to paraphrase the old song, "picking yourself up, dusting yourself off, and starting all over again." If it does, you should hold to the writing standards you've developed over the years, remember your past successes as well as your failures, and send out query letters about your latest book to a new list of editors. If you project a positive attitude, it's likely editors will respond in kind, and you'll soon regain your confidence.

Despite all the vagaries of publishing today, it's still possible to build and sustain a satisfying career in the children's book field. So, whether you're just starting out or are well on your way, take heart. Writing books for children and young people has never been easy, but few other fields of writing are as rewarding. For, unlike many of their adult counterparts, children's books can have a unique and lasting impact on their impressionable young readers. I still remember poring over the illustrations and savoring the words of Wanda Gág's *Millions of Cats*, Robert Lawson's and Munro Leaf's *The Story of Ferdinand*, and Marguerite de Angeli's *Skippack School;* I'm sure you have equally vivid memories of your own childhood favorites.

Not that every children's book that's published assumes the dimensions of a classic; far from it. But who knows? The picture book, nonfiction work, or novel that you're working on today may be enjoyed by thousands of young readers in a few years' time, and still be alive in their memories fifty years from now. Consciously or unconsciously, that's one of the goals most children's book writers aim for—and many achieve it. I hope you will, too.

156

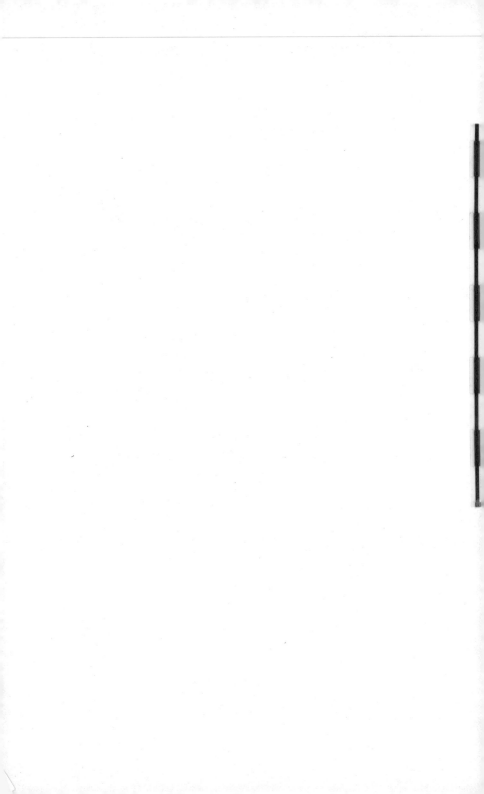